Logic and Reason for the Rest of US:
A Guide to Peace Through Truth

Logic and Reason for the Rest of US: A Guide to Peace Through Truth

Gregory DePetro

Gregory DePetro
2014

First Printing: 2014

ISBN-13:9780692342763

Denuo Publishing
Post Office Box 9652
Laguna Beach, CA 92652

www.LogicandReasonBook.com

Special discounts are available on quantity purchases by corporations, associations, educators, and others. For details, contact the publisher at the above listed address.

Dedication

To all alcoholics, adicts, and sufferers of mental illness I give my love, empathy, compassion and never ending gratitude.

Contents

Acknowledgements

My sincere gratitude, love, and respect to my sister Ashly who is by far my most dedicated supporter and to whom I have always been able to turn in my darkest hours when there seems to be no one else in the world who understand s me.

And also to my sister Nicole who I am so proud of and from whom I gain so much insight.

To my loving mentor and confidant Scott without whom I would not be alive today. Thank you for always being there and being patient.

Preface

When writing a book like this or any book I suppose, as the author you desperately want to be understood by the reader. We all want to be understood and we all want everyone to like us which can make it a challenge to remain completely honest and not worry about offending anyone. The thoughts in this book are controversial and have been mulling around in my head for many years and I have restrained myself on most occasions from sharing them usually to avoid offending someone. When the topics discussed in this book did come up, maybe at a party or just in general conversation, I found myself frustrated trying to express the ideas fully just because the nature of conversation takes many turns and often diverts from the original topic. The philosophies I am sharing in this book are based on a sort of building block understanding and usually required more time to explain than my conversation partner had or wanted to dedicate in that venue. So random ideas I tried to express on a certain topic were usually taken out of context or left unresolved and misunderstood. Ultimately I became so frustrated trying to explain deeply rooted and complex points of view in our world of sound bites and short attention spans that I decided to write it down, and the result is this little book. I don't beat around the bush or pull any punches, I go headlong into topics that most people try to avoid. I didn't want to insult you the reader by filling it up with fluff and verbose explanations just so it would be a bigger book, I used the exact amount of words it took to get my thoughts out, nothing more and nothing less. I've always been bored with the self-indulgent verbosity some authors subject us to in order to make a simple idea seem more complex and important. I attempted to make a point quickly and simply with an economy of words and then move on. I hope that appeals to you and I trust you will get something from your time spent reading this book even if you don't agree with my ideas.

Chapter One
What is Truth?

"The sting of reproach is the truth of it."

-Benjamin Franklin

I'm not writing this book in an effort to convince anyone of any specific truth, or to change anyone's mind about a belief they hold - or to convince anyone to think or believe as I do. This book is simply intended to share my experiences with permeating layers of denial and illogical and irrational thinking. These layers of denial are manifested by subconsciously blocking out obvious facts or fabricating facts. This practice enables us to rationalize and excuse destructive behaviors and beliefs that in hindsight were based on a perceived reality. The behaviors and beliefs I reference in this book are personal to me and some are examples of people with whom I have come in contact. They are only a vehicle through which I am trying to explain the practice of applying logical and reasonable thinking to circumstances in your own life and belief system.

Try to remain open minded if and when I touch on a topic that is personal to you and for which you feel passionately such as religion, politics or traumatic experiences. Understand that these are simply examples to facilitate the application of logical thinking to long-held and deeply rooted beliefs. When the mind is trying to protect itself it quickly becomes defensive and stops listening and can close the door to new ideas, because accepting something as true or not true might force us to accept a list of other truths in a domino effect that we simply are unwilling to accept.

Your willingness and commitment to open mindedness will determine your success in the pursuit of truth. We will examine later how desperately the human mind will hold on to false truth to shield itself from a larger unacceptable truth. But for now I hope that some of you will at the very least use this practice to get closer to truth and to the source of some behaviors and thinking patterns.

 I certainly do not claim to have achieved some higher plateau of self-awareness, in fact, quite the opposite. The more layers of self-deceit I lift and the more epiphanies I have that shatter former beliefs, the more I realize that my current truth is only as firm as the information I have and the information I am willing to accept, and that it could change at any given moment. Does this mean that I am a leaf blowing in the wind, changing my mind at every whimsical thought, subjectively vulnerable to changing circumstances? Absolutely not. This practice has in fact helped me to better understand what drives me and what I accept as truth. It therefore more firmly solidifies my belief system, while always knowing that a new perspective based on new information may be just over the next horizon and could change it. It is a lifelong practice toward an unattainable ideal of achieving self-awareness based on real truth and not fabricated truth.

The word truth as described by the Merriam-Webster dictionary is; "the real facts about something: the things that are true." This definition has the uncanny nature of being very specific and at the same time very ambiguous. It says that truth is things that are true, but isn't what is true open to debate and perception? I will argue in the coming chapters that the answer is no.

I have heard many people say "well, you have your truth and I have my truth, so let's just agree to disagree". That is actually very good interpersonal skills, agreeing to disagree peacefully. But I disagree with the part about me having my truth and you having your truth because it is an illogical and irrational concept. I believe there is only one truth in any given circumstance. People will have their own interpretation of it based on their past experiences and how that truth affects their current belief system. But as we move forward I will lay out my philosophy that as far as Nature is concerned, under the layers of each person's perception, there stands only one truth to be discovered by a person who is willing and able to see it. It only appears different to each of us because of the emotional filters we apply to it.

For example, most people would agree that water conducts electricity. If you saw a broken power line sparking in a pool of water you wouldn't step into the water based on this commonly accepted truth. However, upon closer examination we learn that it is actually the impurities in water that conduct electricity. Pure water, or $H2O$: one molecule of water with two hydrogen atoms covalently bonded to a single oxygen atom, does not conduct electricity. In fact, pure water is an insulator and will not conduct electricity at all. This is a basic example of a truth someone held that can be easily changed with new information. "Oh, I thought water conducted electricity, that's some fun trivia to know and I'll go on with my day now". It doesn't really affect or conflict with any other aspect of their life that would change their self-image so it is easily and readily accepted and can be proved in a lab. But what happens when the so-called truth can't be proved in a lab such as "did my Mother love me?" In both examples the truth exists. It is there and it is not debatable and is based on facts. But how ready are we to accept an unfavorable truth that might affect how we see ourselves?

"The Truth" has always been the truth, and always will be the truth. It is not up for interpretation or manipulation and it is independent of human perception. From a human perspective it is simply most people's goal to get as close to it or as far away from it as suits the result you are trying to achieve. Agreed? Well, be careful about nodding and agreeing too quickly because in this book you will discover how far even you can be from "The Truth". Not your truth, but "The Truth" based on facts, logic and reason.

Logic and Reason for the Rest of Us

Have you ever heard someone describe a horrific childhood where maybe they were beaten by their parents or subjected to malicious, unreasonable punishment or even abandoned? And then they conclude the story with something to the effect of "my parents loved me they just didn't know how to express it"? In this example the reality that this person's mommy and or daddy didn't love them is so unacceptable that the mind will cling to the illusion that they did when it clearly defies all logic and reason. Most likely the parents had mental issues themselves and were incapable of love or had a very warped sense of what it means. But nonetheless the result is irrefutable - that is not how you treat someone you love and therefore they did not love you. And yet the subject excuses the parent's behavior. Why? This reality has so many negative effects on the self-image, such as if my parents didn't love me than I must be unlovable, that the person simply creates a false reality to avoid it. The conscious mind of a person can be told that the mistreatment was not their own fault that a child isn't unlovable, and the person can nod in agreement and say "I know". And yet at the same time the subconscious mind continues to justify relationships with people who treat them poorly because they don't feel worthy of love subconsciously. The conscious mind can intellectualize the concept that it is not their fault and they do deserve to be loved and treated well, but it may take a lot of time and effort to convince the subconscious mind of that simple truth. In some cases they are so convinced of that false reality from an early stage in life that they start acting in a mean and malicious way and actually become someone that is very difficult to love and treat well, substantiating the illusion by making it real.

There is a big difference between your truth and "The Truth". It was the global truth at one point that the planet we live on was flat, which made sense from the limited perspective of the Earth's inhabitants at the time. When we look at a circumstance from within that circumstance we have a very different perspective than when we can see it objectively from the outside and with new information. Thus, from the surface of the Earth with no other perspective it was somewhat logical to assume that the planet was flat and it was considered the truth for a very long time. However in hindsight, it was simply their truth and "The Truth" was later discovered. "The Truth" was always there, it wasn't hiding. It just took a more informed perspective for us to see it. The intention of this book is to help you practice keeping that possibility open. That your truth might not be "The Truth" no matter how important it is to you, how long you've believed it, or how many other people believe it.

The problem most humans have with discovering "The Truth" is that it is usually in conflict with their previous personal truth and thus extremely difficult to accept. "The Truth" didn't change after being discovered. It was always there obeying the laws of physics, logic and reason, it just needed to be discovered by the observer. How often people's personal truth and Nature's truth are in alignment, speaking from personal experience, is very rare. Mostly because within our solitary brains we can decide what our truth is. And when "The Truth" means we would lose something we have or not get something we want, we simply create our own truth to substantiate circumstances allowing us to keep what we have or get what we want. This is a powerful and deceptive ability the human brain possesses, to magically add or ignore so called "facts" to substantiate a preconceived truth. This is why the Star Trek character Spock is so different. He can look at real facts and arrive at a logical truth without the filter of human emotions to warp it.

It is easy to understand and quite reasonable under certain circumstances to knowingly and consciously deceive someone we perceive as a threat. What I find amazing though, is the ability of the human brain to exact this deception upon itself. As if there is an alternate inhabitant of our psyche intentionally tricking us, the enemy within, so to speak. Well, as freaky as it may sound, we do have two distinct inhabitants of our psyche. They have been described in common language as the subconscious and the conscious mind. Most minimally educated people understand and accept the existence of the subconscious mind and the basics of how it can affect thoughts and thus behaviors and habits of the conscious mind. But how motivated are they to fully engage in battle with this powerful force. Yes, I said battle. Seeking out the difference between our truth and "The Truth" is a constant battle against self, and the subconscious self is a formidable and powerful foe because it knows all of our secrets and fears. It is so powerful in fact that many humans have held on to an obviously false truth so much so that it overcomes their own instinct of survival. We can choose, as described earlier, to believe that someone in our life loves us when all logic and reason obviously suggests they don't, because that is a more convenient truth and most likely will not result in our own demise. But imagine how many humans throughout history have held on to a false truth to the point of ending their very existence on this Earth. Addicts, alcoholics, religious fanatics, people who have been abused and terrified are all capable of incredible self-deception and false realities. "The Truth" can be overwhelming and unacceptable, and a false reality is the only way they can survive for periods of time.

This extreme conflict between the subconscious and conscious mind against itself can result in debilitating mental illness. But how many of us practice this same self-deception on a much smaller and less destructive scale every day? People pay unimaginable amounts of money to psychiatrists, psychologists and psychotherapists to assist them in getting their subconscious and conscious mind into a more harmonious alignment. It is up to these professionals to identify the self-deception and guide the conscious mind of the patient to discover this deception their own subconscious mind is perpetrating on them.

At the risk of minimizing a complex and well respected field, that is pretty much my summation of psychotherapy. Most people don't look at it in that context and would simply say they are just trying to figure out why they are so sad, depressed, angry, promiscuous, frightened etc. They believe that they are the victims of an outside force inflicting these things upon them when in fact it is self-inflicted. Sadly a great deal of people who find the courage to initially seek help from a professional never discover "The Truth" because they are only in therapy to prove their truth as being real. If they can convince a trained professional to co-sign their false reality then they can justify it. But there will come a fearful moment in therapy when the subconscious mind realizes the therapist is not substantiating the false truth, and at that moment the conscious mind reluctantly sees a glimpse of "The Truth". It can either find the courage to see the light and have a breakthrough, which is to say it sees through the subconscious mind's deception and forces it to reveal "The Truth", or it can reject "The Truth" and fall back into the more palatable false truth. In the latter case, this is when a person will begin to create excuses why therapy is not working and why they can no longer attend the sessions, leaving the empathetic therapist unable to help the patient. For those of you who have seen the movie "The Matrix", it is the choice between taking the red or green pill. Do you want to retreat back into the blissful ignorance of a false self-image, or are you willing to stay in the uglier reality and fix it and make it beautiful?

There is a clear and distinct divide between the conscious and subconscious mind, like a filter or a two way mirror. The subconscious mind knows "The Truth" and it knows all of our fears and secrets, but it hides things from the conscious mind out of fear. It is up to you, the conscious you that is reading this book, to find the courage to smash those two way mirrors and see what your subconscious is hiding from you.

Logic and Reason for the Rest of Us

Most of us find it difficult to believe that our subconscious is hiding some hidden reality from us. After all it is the same brain isn't it? Yes, it is the same brain that the conscious and subconscious mind occupies, but I believe the divide between the two is a safety mechanism. Sometimes an event or series of events can simply be too overwhelming for a person to absorb and accept immediately, so we have the built in ability to soften the blow by creating a more acceptable temporary version. This gives us time to absorb what happened and slowly come to grips with it. The problem is that some of us never work back toward reality from the temporary more easily accepted version. This is very common in severely traumatic cases, but it is a phenomenon that can occur slowly over time in less dramatic ways to anyone who chooses not accept something they find distasteful. Wait until *your* personal truth is challenged and see how vehemently you will defend it when all logic and reason might dictate that it is in conflict with "The Truth". The Merriam-Webster definition of insanity is: "a deranged state of the mind usually occurring as a specific disorder." I will argue in the coming pages that based on this definition every single human being suffers from at least a mild form of insanity. When the separation of someone's truth and what we collectively know to be "The Truth" is so great we can quickly and easily agree that he or she "has lost touch with reality" or is "insane" by our own standards. But what happens if I raise the standard? We are quick to accept our own insane thinking such as "I don't know why I keep doing this" whatever "this" is. But we do know why we keep doing it. It is just buried in the subconscious under layers of denial, rationalizations and fear. And so we live in a "deranged state of the mind" repeating the same self-destructive patterns over and over trying to substantiate a false reality however mild it may be.

Chapter Two
Deceit and why we use it.

"Children always understand. They have open minds. They have built-in shit detectors."

-Madonna

From the beginning of time man has practiced the art of deception, and we are not the only species to do so. I'm sure there was a caveman who was asked if he had extra food in his cave and he responded "no", or grunted to that effect, to make sure he and his kin had enough. Deception is based on the natural instinct of fear, as described in the previous chapter, fear of losing what we have or not getting what we want. It is that simple, and I encourage you not to complicate it any more than that.

I will repeat it for effect; *all deception, especially self-deception, is based in fear of losing something we have or not getting something we want.*

The convolution and complexity comes into play when you add in all of the possibilities of what people are subconsciously afraid of losing or not getting and why. It can be an extreme, such as the psychopath who kills women because he is trying to get the illusion of control his torturous mother took from him in childhood. Or it can be minimal such as an employee taking home office supplies for personal use justifying it by thinking that he is not getting paid enough so it's only fair and not stealing, and every variation between the two. Conscious deception is less of a challenge to correct because we see it and admit we are doing it. And as we all know, it is only possible to fix a problem we are aware of or accept as a problem. Simply put, a habitual liar has a better chance of curbing the bad behavior than someone still in denial of the deception because he admits he is doing it. However, even conscious deception is not an easy behavior to stop because it is still compensating for a subconscious void created by denial of "The Truth". The lying is the symptom, not the problem.

Telling someone with a gun pointed at you anything they want to hear in order to survive is perfectly understandable deception, and most people wouldn't blame you for it. But it is still an extreme example of how all deception is based in fear of losing something we have, in this case life, or not getting something we want. It is my opinion that this is a law of the universe as true as Einstein's theory of relativity. I know I keep beating this dead horse, but I can't express how important it is to accept that simple point of view if you endeavor to seek the root of the motivations for all of your actions and thus move closer to "The Truth". What am I afraid of losing or not getting in this circumstance and how is it affecting my actions? In the case of having a gun pointed at you I would encourage you to do whatever you need to in order to survive. This could mean being completely honest or practicing the most convincing deception you are capable of. However, philosophically speaking, if everyone practiced the art of what I am advocating in this book, that circumstance would be extremely rare or nonexistent. Yes, that is an idealistic view, and considering human history, pretty unlikely to happen within the next 100 years, but follow me for a moment. In order to make a point I ask you to think about why a person would be holding a gun on another person. Not the immediate reason, but the root of the reason. What chain of circumstantial events over a lifetime, or even generations of lifetimes, could have led to one person pointing a gun at another person? Whoever is wrong or right in the infinite possibilities of reasons, I assure you it is rooted in fear and deception and would have been organically avoided if all people applied logic, reason, and self-honesty in all aspects of their life. Is that too simplistic, idealistic, and unbelievable? Absolutely, it is human nature to feel fear and react with deception and will most likely never be removed from the human experience, but once again extreme examples are used to make a point. We will revisit this theory about organically avoiding conflict as a species by removing fear based on deception at the end of the book. Certainly it is not my belief that this little book should inspire a species to a utopian existence. But the objectivity of the big picture by use of extreme examples should help you see how we might move in that direction.

Let's look at how you and I, to one degree or another, project a less than true image of who we are through deception. Not only to the world, but most importantly to ourselves, and thus create fear of being found out. When we deceive ourselves with our subconscious mind and others with our conscious mind, we are creating a false image like the Wizard of Oz behind the curtain, always afraid someone will discover the curtain and pull it away exposing our true selves to all. When someone else discovers "The Truth" about us we too are reluctantly forced to see it, and we will go to great lengths to ensure that doesn't happen. Therein lays the root of human conflict. The saddest part is that deep down we are all afraid of the same fundamental things. It is only our fear of sharing those fears with each other that divides us. We believe our fears to be vulnerabilities and if discovered they will be used against us. The irony is that our fears themselves are not vulnerabilities, the vulnerability is manufactured by us when we attempt to conceal them. The deeper damage done by this practice is that in concealing our fears we enable ourselves to avoid facing them. Thankfully, most of our fears are just bogeymen and when confronted and faced are defeated with much less effort than we imagined. So when we conceal our fears, we not only empower others to exploit them, we empower the fear as well.

How many of us at some point have been caught in a lie or even a little fib? Maybe we accidentally contradict ourselves and thus reveal an obvious lie and find ourselves in that sudden panic at a party with our friends all looking at us waiting for us decide what to do about it.

Logic and Reason for the Rest of Us

There we are, frozen in a moment of truth with our brains racing for a way out, searching for a way to avoid the curtain being pulled back on our deception. Maybe we let out a big breath and laugh and say "OK, you got me, I just didn't want you all to know blah blah blah" and everyone laughs and moves on with the moment. You feel a sudden relief and almost a peace in that you will no longer have to concern yourself with maintaining that deception no matter how small or large it was. And the wonderful, undeniable result in most cases is that we feel just a little bit closer to the people we were honest with and them to us. Humans find a certain comfort in commonality no matter how big or small it is. Revealing these things about ourselves draws us closer because others can say "I too didn't want anyone to know blah blah blah about me either, thanks for being honest".

Another outcome might be that, like so many of us will do in that moment of panic, you choose to blindly defend the obvious lie with irrational distorted facts. Maybe the fear is just too much to overcome and you are not able to reveal yourself to that audience. So you stick to your guns and deny obvious truths and distort facts to substantiate the lie. You become even more embarrassed as you dig yourself deeper and deeper. This makes it increasingly more difficult to come clean because now you have defended the lie with increasing effort. In most cases people will not aggressively continue to call you out and they eventually let you off the hook and nod to each other in silent agreement that you are a dishonest person. How does that feel? Come on, you remember it, we've all been there at one point or another. We can go so far as to almost convince ourselves of the lie even though all logic and reason debunks it. The sad result is we withdraw further from those people into the isolation of deceit. Guilt creeps in even if we deny its existence and we find ourselves having to create even more lies to back that one up. The worst part of this is that it gets easier and easier to lie as we begin to build this web of deception.

How many times have we all heard the statement "thanks for being honest"? Why do we feel gratitude when someone is honest with us, even if it is a seemingly insignificant issue? Because dishonesty is based in fear and thus creates fear. If someone fears us enough to lie we most likely have a reason to fear them. Conversely, if someone trusts us enough to be honest then we can most likely trust them relative to the degree of honesty in that particular circumstance. Con artists use that technique all the time, revealing a falsely embarrassing truth or vulnerability to gain our confidence. We usually don't analyze things to that degree, but if you think about it, isn't that where that sense of comfort and safety comes from when someone is honest with us?

In many cases the cycle of deception begins very young and is the result of being raised and influenced by people who practice the same deception. As a result we find ourselves in a world of people all perpetuating false truths so no one else finds out that they are just as afraid and insecure as we are. These small deceptions build over time into an overall false presentation of who we really are because we want social acceptance and respect or we're afraid of losing social acceptance or respect. This creates a feeling of insecurity within us, meaning we are not secure or comfortable with ourselves because who we really are is hiding behind the false image we project to the outside world.

Let's discuss that word; Insecure. It is thrown around high schools and offices everywhere, we learn it very young and accuse everyone of being guilty of it at some point. What is insecurity? It's exactly what I described in the previous paragraphs. It has many varying degrees from the mild to the debilitating, but is all based in the fear of being found out that our inside doesn't match our outside and that our deception will be discovered. As we begin to bring our inside into harmony and alignment with our outside, or vice versa, a natural byproduct of that action occurs. We lose the fear of being found out because there is little or nothing to hide and this is called self-confidence. Easier said than done I know, but that has been one of the most rewarding results of my journey. Just the peace of not living in fear of being found out because there is nothing I am afraid of anyone finding out. Of course I have things that I would prefer weren't common knowledge, but if they did become common knowledge it wouldn't affect how I feel about myself. Because just as a byproduct of living as honestly and as close to "The Truth" as I can, I have slowly gained humility and self-confidence. And as a result I have reduced how much what other people think of me affects how I think of myself. That is the reward we seek in this journey.

The peace I describe is sometimes difficult to accept at first because the drama our deception causes is often a source of excitement in our lives. This is difficult to accept for most people because when said out loud it sounds ridiculous. "I want peace in my life. Don't tell me I create turmoil in my life because it's exciting, I have real issues to deal with." I know it sounds silly, but have you ever been watching a movie or a TV sitcom and thought "if he just told her the truth in the beginning she would have understood and this whole stupid situation would've been avoided"? But then we wouldn't have a show. Well, that rings just as true in real life, but we love the drama don't we? We don't like to admit it, but of course we do, there is an entire multi-billion dollar industry that entertains us with it every day. The dramatic complexity of human deceit based in fear is exciting. The desire for drama is so innate in some people that when they are recovering from an addiction like alcoholism, drug addiction, gambling, physically abusive relationships and so on, and their life begins to calm down because the addiction is being curbed, they subconsciously begin to create drama in their life because they miss it. We can actually be more comfortable in turmoil than in peace. Sometimes we have to learn how to live in peace after having lived in dramatic conflict for so long.

I grew up in an alcoholic household where there was very little honesty and openness about feelings. We learned quickly that the embarrassing things that happen inside the house should be kept inside the house. We learn to lie, rationalize and excuse insane behavior and as we grow up and become adult children of alcoholics we find ourselves lying even when the truth would serve us better. It becomes a habit. I gained a lot of insight into my subconscious psyche after reading Janet Woititz's book "Adult Children of Alcoholics" and I recommend it to anyone who grew up in an alcoholic or addict household.

The practice of deceit and fear of being found out is passed down from generation to generation and is a serious challenge to undo. I can attest to the difficulty myself when I hit bottom at the hands of my own alcoholism. I realized I had to completely tear down and rebuild my perception of myself, the world, and my place in it. Alcohol for me was the symptom, not the problem. For the sake of survival in my case, I needed to accept the world as it really is, try to be as honest with myself as possible and begin getting my truth in line with "The Truth". I had to enlist the help of a selfless and dedicated mentor. I agreed to share everything about myself with him in order that he could guide me through the web of self-deception that I had woven my entire life. I had created a warped self-image based on my excuses, rationalizations, and good intentions. But I needed to see myself as who I truly was based on my actions if I was going to fix the problems. I learned that a person is the sum of their actions, not their intentions and excuses, and that is a tough pill to swallow in many cases. It can in fact be too tough a pill to swallow for some, and thus many of my brother and sister sufferers will carry the denial to the grave. Like the person holding onto the rock at the bottom of the lake because the rock is all they know and they are unwilling to let go of it.

For most of you, self-deception isn't the looming sickle of the Grim Reaper like it is with alcoholics and addicts. Perhaps your release comes in other forms like over spending, promiscuity, anger, control issues, failing relationships - the list goes on and on. Or perhaps you just simply endeavor to improve your self-awareness. In any case it is my belief that the human experience on Earth is only to improve emotionally and spiritually as best we can. All material and relational things on this Earth are simply props to facilitate that growth. Sadly, so many of us get caught in the pitfall of seeing the props as the purpose and not the means to the purpose. They seek to achieve short term comfort even if that comfort is an illusion and the result of false truths. The pursuit of self-awareness creates discomfort which most people want to avoid. Our time on this Earth is not to be spent avoiding discomfort but seeking it out, because it is only through discomfort that we grow. If it were not for discomfort we would all still be living in well decorated caves, and ironically that is exactly what a lot of people are doing with their lives. When I say "seek out discomfort" fundamentally I mean seek out "The Truth" and acknowledge it. For instance, if we treat someone poorly we can seek to remain comfortable by simply justifying and excusing it and maybe avoiding that person. Or we can seek out discomfort by admitting "The Truth" of our mistake or deception to ourselves and facing the person with an honest and heartfelt apology, even if the person is a jerk. Actually, it is even better if the person is a jerk, because that is more uncomfortable and thereby creates more humility and thus more emotional and spiritual growth. The battle against self is the feeling you will experience when trying to avoid that discomfort. It is the battle against pride and ego and the fear of losing social status even if that status is based upon false truths. The biggest irony is that through those moments of discomfort that we seek out and overcome, we move closer to real comfort as the result of alleviating guilt, shame and remorse. I encourage you to always seek out short term discomfort to achieve long term peace. But I digress and need to get back to why we use deception in our everyday lives, as I will address the solution in later chapters.

As discussed earlier, there are two distinct inhabitants of our psyche, the conscious mind and the subconscious mind, and the line between them is murky. What I mean is that on one hand we have the deceptions we perpetrate knowingly and consciously with a clear and understood fear. Such an example could be a closeted homosexual fearing the social repercussions of their sexuality, or a criminal fearing being caught and prosecuted. These are clear and conscious deceptions that we are aware of and of course the list goes on and on. On the other hand we have the deep subconscious deceptions that we are not consciously aware of. Such as a hyper vigilant fear of the world based on a traumatic experience or experiences in childhood that we either remember or have blocked out. These deceptions live deep in our subconscious and affect us without us being consciously aware of them. But somewhere in the middle there are the lies we have told ourselves and others for so long that we actually begin to believe them on some level. These deceptions are the ones that live in the murkiness between the conscious and the subconscious. The lies we hear ourselves telling again and again while inside our head we're actually trying to remember if they are true or not.

So why does the human brain deceive itself on so many levels? In short, the answer is to create a false version of the world that it can accept, which rationalizes the actions it takes to protect itself from real or perceived threats. You might want to read the previous sentence again, but that's pretty much it.

Logic and Reason for the Rest of Us

Even the conscious lies of the criminal are based in subconscious rationalizations. It is my opinion that every action a person carries out, they believe to be righteous in the moment they are doing it even if they know it is wrong. Did I just contradict myself? At first glance yes, but let's look a little deeper. I know that robbing a bank is wrong and against the law. I know it is other people's money and I know I am not supposed to take other people's money. However if I decide to do it I need to make it right in my mind. Every action someone takes has to be the right action in their mind at that time or the mind wouldn't do it. I might convince myself that the bank has insurance and so the people will not lose their money. Or I might rationalize that the world is not fair and I have been denied my fair chance at earning that money so it is my right to take what I have been denied by society.

Sometimes the ability to make an action right in our mind is very brief in the heat of passion. Then shortly after it is done we can no longer sustain the rationalization and we consciously realize we were wrong. This is called "temporary insanity" and is a legal defense in the U.S. Judicial System. For example, a person comes home and finds their spouse having sex with their neighbor. He or she may be so overwhelmed with anger and rage that in the heat of the moment of feeling deceived and wronged they could justify that the spouse and the neighbor "deserve to be killed" for their crime. In that state of mind they could pick up a gun and carry out that justified death sentence. Shortly after the act they may come back to their senses and realize the permanent repercussions of their actions and the "wrongness" of it and feel remorse. Some juries will accept that as a reasonable defense because in that moment of rage the act was justified and right. If it wasn't somehow justified, short term or long term, they wouldn't have been able to do it.

I believe the less gratuitous practice of self-deception is a form of temporary insanity as well. It may not be resulting in egregious illegal behavior, or maybe it is, and it is sustained for much longer periods of time, such as an entire lifetime. In either case, the mind that commits any action at all believes at the time it is committing it that the action is right. The human mind will never commit a wrong action; it must first convince itself that something is right before it can do it. If "The Truth" stands in the way of seeing what it wants to do as right, it simply creates an alternate truth to justify the action. The trick is to be ever vigilant in questioning your perception and your motives. You must learn to set aside the fear of losing what you have or not getting what you want, and act on "The Truth" not your version of it.

All humans are born with the natural instinctual understanding of what is wrong or right in any given circumstance, it's just hidden beneath layers of self-deception. It is an instinct. Let's call it the "instinct of truth". Instincts are extremely difficult to explain when you really think about it. Just look at a turtle that hatches from an egg and knows he should scurry to the ocean as soon as possible. How could that turtle by all logic and reason know that it should run to the ocean? Think about that for a moment. We just accept it because it happens, we know it happens and so, well, there it is. But think about how impossible it really seems that this turtle, never before having existed and seen the Earth, would know to come out of its shell and immediately run to the ocean with no opportunity to have learned that practice. And yet they all do it, every single one of them.

We will get into applying logic and reason to this discussion of instincts later, but for now I am illustrating that instincts are real and do exist at some level for all creatures. It is like the basic operating system of a computer without which you could turn the power on but the computer wouldn't understand itself or be ready to carry out any functions. It requires a basic operating system to "boot up" and then we can install programs and it can learn the functions we want it to perform. Instincts are the basic operating systems of all living creatures without which we wouldn't continue to breathe when we fell asleep, to eat when our bodies needed food, to procreate or to run to the ocean when we come out of our shells. So, however difficult it is to explain I believe all humans are born with instincts, one of which is the "instinct of truth". The ability to know wrong from right in every single little circumstance they face every day. What makes it difficult for us to see is the self-deception that begins very young and builds slowly over time into layers upon layers of excuses and rationalizations. It begins the first time a baby learns that when it cries it gets fed. From the first moment it cries for attention even when it's not hungry, the act of deception begins to be perfected.

In my own experience working with my mentor to systematically untangle the web of self-deception I had spent a lifetime weaving, I became aware of the "Instinct of Truth" within me. I recall on every occasion I came to him with a seeming dilemma that I thought required the Wisdom of Solomon to figure out, it ended up that I knew the right answer deep down all along. "The Truth" lay within me and at my disposal to apply if I only chose to acknowledge it. So why wouldn't I choose to acknowledge it? That's right, because "The Truth" meant I would lose something I had or not get something I wanted. My truth enabled me to keep what I had or to get what I wanted - my truth being based on excuses, rationalizations, and a childish sense of entitlement.

This practice is seen in the sandboxes of pre-schools to the highest levels of elected office and boardrooms of industry. It is the exact same behavior only to varying degrees of complexity and import. My mentor, not being a genius as far as I know, and not being a licensed psychiatrist, simply used his own experiences to ask the difficult questions. Through this process we systematically lifted the layers of self-deception I had applied to the circumstance until I revealed "The

Truth" to myself. "The Truth" that was there all along at the root of the situation. Once I was guided to acknowledge it I knew it had been there the entire time. After fifteen years of practicing this, I have become very adept at checking my true motives in most circumstances, and they are usually not what I thought they were at first glance. In a constant battle against self I still can fool myself after all these years into justifying excuses to get what I want or not lose what I have. And so I still benefit from running things by my mentor. I heard someone say once that their mentor is someone who questions their answers, not answers their questions.

It is a lifelong practice toward a perfect ideal of self-awareness that we will never achieve. But the journey is amazing and rewarding and nothing is better than passing it on as I have tried to do many times and what I attempt to do with this book. But once again I digress. Allow me to get back to the topic of why we deceive ourselves.

I have done some acting and trained in some great acting classes and studios, and as of today I'm sure you have not seen me in anything. However the training I received as an actor was extremely revealing. For instance I learned that to portray a character accurately you cannot judge the character. Your judgment of the character will unconsciously come through in your performance and make it inauthentic, like it or not. Armed with this information I was cast to play a serial rapist murderer. I found myself faced with the dilemma of having to understand his rationalization for what he does so I am not judging him while portraying him. How can I try to understand one of the most revolting horrific acts a human can do to another? I started to study what motivates these people and their common backgrounds and modus operandi. What could happen to a human brain that could somehow allow it to rationalize committing these acts? As I immersed myself in this world of the highly disturbed mind of a serial rapist murderer, I found myself understanding to some small degree, the pain and trauma they were subjected to as a source of their own desire to inflict pain and trauma. There are many motivations these people feel, one of which is to simply regain temporary control that they believe was taken from them. Obviously I am not excusing that behavior, but beginning on some level to understand it is terrifying. Subsequently the funding for the film didn't come through and the film was never made. The experience however, left me with some disturbing insight into how deep and convincing rationalization and false reality can go, and the horrific potential results. Once again, in this extreme case of mental illness, even the mind of the serial killer rapist has convinced itself that these actions are right and justified.

On the other side of such a crime, the mind of the rape victim often fabricates deception upon itself to deal with the trauma as well. It is my understanding that many rape victims suffer a great feeling of loss of control after being raped. The safety they believed they had before the crime is diminished and control over their own destiny they thought they had is also diminished. The human mind wants to gain those things back somehow, even if it is a false sense of those feelings. So the subconscious mind of some rape victims rationalizes promiscuity as a response which may give the conscious mind the feeling that they are in control of sex and not the threatening men. Or in some cases the subconscious mind will begin to over eat into obesity in order to make themselves less attractive prey to the predator. Both of these responses are committed by the subconscious mind in an effort to protect itself and restore what was taken from it.

So how does a psychotherapist slowly guide this person toward reality and the source of this destructive behavior when the subconscious mind is using it to cope with an unacceptable truth? That is the art of therapy and why there are good ones, bad ones, and great ones. It takes patience (pun intended) and is a slow process of revealing to the conscious mind what it can handle at any given moment without shocking it into further retreat from "The Truth". This is why a good therapist asks questions instead of telling you what the deception is. Questions are the only way to let the conscious mind decide for itself what truth it is ready to accept at any given point. Like a staircase from darkness the subconscious mind knows the journey required, but the conscious mind can only stand to look at one or several steps at a time. In the beginning of my own journey toward "The Truth", if someone had told me all of what would be required and the depth of my self-deception, it would have seemed insurmountable and I probably wouldn't have taken the first step. I describe it as a magic pool, where as soon as I believe I have arrived at self-awareness and understanding of my true motivations, the bottom drops out to reveal a deeper layer of self-deception and so on and so on. The human brain is like a computer, there is a distinct reason for everything it does. The challenge is to sift through the complex program to find the faulty code and fix it, because no human action is random and pointless.

For those of you who are not so deeply disturbed as to have become a murderer or rapist, and if you are lucky enough to not have been so severely victimized, let's look at how the exact same deception is being perpetrated by your subconscious minds to a lesser degree. What secrets is your subconscious mind hiding from you that manifest themselves in destructive behaviors from the mild to the debilitating?

There are certain characteristics that are commonly accepted as negative by society such as selfishness, vengefulness, vanity, dishonesty, and allowing what other people think of us to determine our own self-image etc. How many times have you heard people say "I don't care what people think of me"? How many times have you said it yourself? Almost no one I have ever met will consciously admit that they care deeply about, and thus base many decisions, good or bad, on what others think of them. No one wants to consciously admit that they act selfishly or are dishonest. No one wants to admit that they punish based on vengeance instead of teaching, but we do it all the time and deny it to ourselves with a false reality. If you want to see idealistic self-perceptions, just go to any dating web site and read the autobiographical profiles. If all of those profiles were accurate self-appraisals there would be millions more happy and harmonious relationships in the world than there are. And the scariest part of all is that most of them actually believe their description of themselves despite all evidence to the contrary. It is amazing to witness a brain contradict itself in the same thought and simply skip over the missing fact that would make the contradiction clear. Like a skilled movie editor cutting out a line of dialog and piecing it together to form another effect.

Here's an example; I was discussing a circumstance with a rational and intelligent person whom I respect very much where the topic was whether or not someone should keep secret a minor surgery they had to correct a small physical defect in a private area of their body. The short recovery was going to limit activity and most likely would illicit questions as to why the activity was being limited and this person suggested making up an excuse. They stated that "some things are just private". I asked why that should be kept private when it was no fault of the person getting the corrective surgery and would have no lasting effect on them. They replied again that "it just wasn't for other people to know". I asked "so you're afraid of what people will think?" The reply; "I don't care what people think, it's just that some things should just be kept private." I said "but that's a contradiction; if something so minor should be kept private it could only be because we care what other people will think." The response again was "I don't care what people think, it should just be kept private."

The point of whether or not you agree or disagree that it should or shouldn't be kept private is irrelevant. The point here is how an otherwise intelligent and rational brain could contradict itself in an attempt to ignore and deny the clear fact that the motivation of the deception was to avoid what other people would think. We have been programmed to believe that caring what other people think is a bad thing and is a distasteful characteristic to have, so the brain simply creates a false reality to justify the action and ignore the motivation. If a person admits "yes I care what other people will think and so I will keep this private" they might be forced by admitting it to ask themselves why they care what other people think. This might reveal the false image they are trying to project based on a small degree of insecurity. "The Truth" in this case is so distasteful that they simply ignore it even when it results in an obvious contradiction in logic and reason.

This example could be considered a minor, and by most people's standards, an irrelevant deception that will have no negative effects in the grand scheme of life. I disagree. This is a small manifestation of how we create and present a false image to the world based in fear. This example when joined with many other small manifestations of fear builds into a larger differential between our inside and our outside. If this person makes up an excuse why they have to limit their activity, they have now manufactured, of their own making, a reason to fear being found out. And we know from our earlier discussion that this feeling creates distance from our fellows and adds to the isolation of deception. Yes, this is small and you may think I am splitting hairs here, but an example like this becomes just one thread in The Wizard of OZ's curtain.

Just like our silly TV sitcoms, if they simply tell their friends why they have to limit their activity, even if there is a little embarrassment initially, they avoid the drama of deception. They gain confidence by being true to themselves, and they earn the trust of their fellows which brings them closer. But the most important thing is that they have no fear of being found out because there is nothing being hidden. Honesty equals peace of mind. The title of this chapter is "Deceit and why we use it". Our subconscious mind deceives us, and our conscious mind deceives others simply out of fear of losing something we have or not getting something we want.

Chapter Three
The Internal Judge, Jury and Executioner

"Your worst enemy cannot harm you as much as your own unguarded thoughts."

-Buddha

We looked at the difference between our perceived truth and The Universe's actual truth. We also looked at some of the reasons we create our false truth either consciously or subconsciously and what we stand to gain from doing it. There are undeniable short term benefits of deception, such as deceiving someone out of money or property, and in some cases this can lead to great wealth and prestige. But based on my theory of our built in "instinct of truth" which is always there buried under layers of rationalization, we will ultimately never allow ourselves to find true happiness and contentment under these circumstances. In this case we have made the props of this world the purpose of our life and thus are left empty and unfulfilled among our material fortune.

That is not to say that there is anything wrong with wealth or abundance. If it is acquired honestly and used wisely there is great peace and joy that can be found. My point here is that whatever we gain through deception and means that we subconsciously know to be wrong will never bring us true peace and joy. Whether it is the local guy who has the envy of everyone on his block, or the billionaires of global notoriety, the inescapable guilt never allows us to be truly happy and peaceful. Our "Instinct of Truth" sentences us to this self-inflicted punishment handed down by our own internal judge. You will find many such people who seem to be "living it up" and would laugh at this philosophy. They might sternly and defiantly say they did what they had to do to succeed and they feel fine about it. But behind closed doors you will ultimately find unexplainable anger, emotional emptiness and loneliness, broken or unhealthy relationships, even suicide. And they won't see that they are doing it to themselves. The subconscious guilt that lives deep under layers of excuses and rationalizations, whether consciously acknowledged or not, will not be ignored. Whether poor or wealthy beyond belief, you can tell if someone's heart is truly happy, joyful and free and you can tell if it is not. Even if they appear at the moment to be wallowing in the material rewards, "The Truth" will always win out.

I was lucky enough to have made the acquaintance of a self-made multi-millionaire who succeeded by honest hard work and ingenuity. He used a portion of that wealth to start a foundation to help underprivileged children get access to education and opportunities they otherwise would have missed. I can tell you I have never seen such true happiness, joy and peace in a person's eyes as his. So make no mistake, my point has nothing to do with poverty or wealth in and of itself being evil. Simply that the human brain will never accept true peace and happiness while it feels guilt shame and remorse. Even if that guilt shame and remorse is buried deeply in the subconscious.

Maybe you have been struggling to understand the source of some self-destructive behavior. Or maybe you have witnessed a loved one or friend exhibiting these behaviors and wondered why in the world someone would do these things to themselves. Based on my own journey through the highs and lows of life and endeavoring to always improve self-awareness, I came to this realization; when we see a self-destructive person systematically destroying the good things they have in life, what we are witnessing is a person who has accidentally exceeded their own self-image and is subconsciously correcting for it.

We will always, in our deepest subconscious selves, make sure we have exactly what we believe we deserve. When I didn't like who I was and the way I treated people, even though it was buried in rationalizations, I would always "wait for the other shoe to drop" when something good happened to me. I'm a pretty smart and capable guy so despite myself I would occasionally bring good fortune into my life. But I knew it would be short lived because I was "such an unlucky person." Only when I changed my actions and became a man that I could love and respect did I feel comfortable with the blessings I receive in life. Only then did I start to see that all of my "bad luck" was of my own making. My subconscious internal judge was passing sentence on me for my guilt and punishing me without my conscious mind being aware of it. Ultimately the outside will always come to reflect the inside, no matter how many material assets we use to camouflage it.

Have you ever read about a celebrity destroying their lives, or actually ending their lives, and found yourself asking "why would they do that, they had everything you could want in life?" The truth is they had empty props and little or nothing of true value that life has to offer. In fact wealth and celebrity in most cases exacerbates that fact. It can create an even more profound false image projected to the world and thus a deeper isolation and despair. The scary part is when you achieve all the things you believed would give you peace and happiness and you are faced with the terrifying reality that they don't, it is devastating and creates the sense of hopelessness. If you are not a person of great material means you can continue to lean on the false hope that you could win the lottery and all your problems would be over. But when you have those things and still feel empty and lost there is no apparent hope. Whether wealthy, poor, famous, or anonymous, the law of the universe is, well, universal. Deception is based in fear and creates isolation and thus more fear, and no material or physical things will offer true long term relief. Once again this is not to say that fame and fortune is bad in and of itself. It is very rare, but there are wealthy famous people who have navigated the pitfalls and use their fame and wealth for good things while maintaining an accurate self-image and are quite peaceful and content.

If it is true that we will subconsciously make sure that in the end we have exactly what we believe we deserve, then that means that we are responsible for our situation even if we feel we are a victim of it. As you have probably figured out by now, I like to use extreme examples to make a point. I am going to hit you over the head with one here that touches on a very sensitive subject. You may see through the initial reaction and accept my point or you may think I am an insensitive jerk who doesn't understand the complexity of these situations, but in any case, here we go.

Let's look at the abused woman living either in a trailer park or a mansion being physically and emotionally abused by a husband or boyfriend. How could she possibly be inflicting this situation upon herself based on my theory that she is subconsciously making sure she gets exactly what she believes she deserves? Not what she deserves, but what she believes she deserves. It's certainly not her fault this guy is an animal, and she may be terrified into staying for fear of her or her children's lives, and justifiably so. But let's look at the circumstances that might have led to this predicament. She was most likely raised with low self-esteem as a result of poor parenting. Even if she was a good person based on her actions and genuine concern for other people, she most likely has a very low self-image for a variety of possible reasons. How can I be sure of this? Because I know that no one with healthy self-esteem and a good self-image would tolerate even the earliest first indications of an abusive partner, even if he was at first very charming. There had to be the first time when the controlling abusive behavior became apparent and at that moment the person decides if this is acceptable or if it is not based on how they feel about themselves. Now I am completely aware that there are obsessive people who can become stalkers even after one date and that is obviously a different circumstance and not relative to what I am describing. I am also aware that there can be many variations of circumstances that I can't simplify into one example, but sadly what I am describing here is very typical. Almost every woman has at some point encountered a jerk who fancied her. There are the women who simply don't tolerate it and move on until they find someone who treats them well, and of course there are the ones who seem to just go from one jerk to another and wonder why. The answer is that we are responsible for the people we attract and the people we are attracted to. As a result we ultimately end up with exactly what we believe we deserve in our subconscious image of ourselves. This could be because when we were children we witnessed or were the victim of abuse, or because of deep guilt for some bad things we did, but in any case we accept what we feel we deserve. So you may be asking "is it this woman's fault that she was raised with a poor self-image and low self-esteem and thus accepted abusive treatment and ended up in this situation?" No, it isn't, and it is all too common and very sad, but who is at fault is not my point here. The point is that whatever the reason is that she feels she deserves this treatment, she believes she does. Deep down under layers of denial and self-pity she feels she is getting exactly what she deserves. Once again, not what she actually deserves, but what her low self-image makes her believe she deserves. The day she wakes up and says to herself, "I don't deserve this", and truly means it in her conscious and subconscious mind, will be the day she begins to change her situation to one her new self-image believes she deserves. This example can be subject to millions of variations and circumstances and can be interchangeable with women, men, rich, poor, etc., but it will ring true in almost all of them. Ultimately we end up with exactly what we feel we deserve. Not what we actually deserve, but what we believe we deserve.

We can just as easily look at the abusive husband or boyfriend and apply the same truth. Why is he abusive and controlling? What circumstances led to his self-image and thus his abusive behavior? I am as sure in this circumstance as with the woman that it is based in low self-esteem and poor self-image. Maybe he was raised in an abusive home or no home at all, and maybe he witnessed a woman being abused and learned no respect for women. It is likely he was, on some level, made to feel small, stupid, weak, unimportant, or not in control. Feeling those things he may have compensated for his fear and feelings of inadequacy by controlling someone weaker than him. Maybe it's not that dramatic, and the feelings of low self-esteem are milder and so there is no physical abuse. It might be more of an emotional abuse in the form of belittling and controlling behaviors. Either way it stems from fear of being found out that the outside doesn't match the inside. The man doesn't feel like someone who is worthy of love or like a person who someone would want to be with so he is in constant fear that she will find someone who is. His obvious response is to belittle other men to prove that no one else is more worthy than him, and to belittle her so she feels she is not worthy of someone better. He limits her exposure to other people who might contradict the image he is imposing on her and to limit the chances she might encounter the "better man". Of course this is all happening in his subconscious mind, desperately ignoring the "instinct of truth" that is deep within him. He creates rationalizations and excuses why she deserves it and why it is for her own good.

So how did these two people find each other? It's no accident, it happens simply by the process of elimination. I'm sure at some point he was attracted to successful women with good self-esteem who were self-supportive and happy. But at the first sign of his controlling belittling tendencies these women moved on. They know who they are and they're not going to let him make them feel bad about themselves. I'm also sure at some point she was attracted to good guys who tried to treat her well by respecting her and telling her she was beautiful and buying flowers and opening doors for her. But she didn't believe it because she doesn't feel worthy of those things because of her low self-image. She thinks they're being insincere and dishonest because they are obviously lying when they're complimenting her, aren't they? They both get caught in the same horrible trap of asking themselves whenever they happen to meet someone with a healthy self-image; "if this person is with me, what's wrong with them?" That is an unwinnable conundrum and self-destructive pattern which always has the same result. Ultimately they sabotage relationships with healthy people until one day they meet each other and fulfill each other's self-image perfectly. They end up with exactly what they subconsciously believe they deserve. They continue to blame each other, or their parents, or the world for their unhappiness and thus perpetuate the life they subconsciously feel they deserve. They create the self-fulfilling prophecy.

You may be impressed with my insight, or you may think I'm an idiot who is simply regurgitating basic psychology 101 principals. But what I hope you will see is that if basic logic and reason is applied to any circumstance with real self-honesty, the answer comes into focus clearly. We see that it was always within us, and only then do we have a chance at correcting the root problem and not the symptoms. The challenge is that if we do that, we subsequently have to stop blaming others and take responsibility for ourselves, and that is not easy to do.

Here is a concept to chew on; one of the most powerful instincts of the human mind, second only to the instinct of survival, is the desire to be right. Not right as in "I'm right and you're wrong" in a disagreement or argument, but that the mind's perception of the world and a particular belief system is right. If the mind believes the world to be an unsafe place it will do everything in its power to prove that to be true by seeing what it wants to see and disregarding facts to the contrary. If the mind believes that people are dishonest, it will do everything in its power to prove that to be true, and so on and so on. Whatever a set of experiences has brought us to conclude, whether it is true or not, our subconscious mind will go to unbelievable lengths to substantiate that belief. That is the root of the self-fulfilling prophecy. If a woman believes that all men are dishonest and cheaters, she will never trust and always question "where were you? Who was that woman? Why didn't you call me?" until one day he decides he doesn't deserve this treatment and leaves. Then she can say "see, I told you he was a liar when he said he loved me, and he probably left me for another woman" thus creating the self-fulfilling prophecy to substantiate that preconceived belief. The self-fulfilling prophecy can make you feel like a fortune teller because it always comes true.

Have you ever read Edgar Allen Poe's The Raven? It is a poem about a raven that flies into a man's house and says the word "nevermore". That's all it ever says, and the man's subconscious mind learns very quickly that that is all it can say. So what does the depressed lonely man do? He asks the raven questions knowing what the answer will be. He does this to substantiate his depressed view of the world. He asks if he will ever see his lost love Lenore, "quote the raven "nevermore". The insight into this dark part of the human psyche, and the ability to construct it into beautiful prose, is what made Poe the genius he was.

Another great example Poe left us is "The Tell Tale Heart". (Spoiler alert) It is about a madman who murders a person and buries the dismembered body under his floorboards. While being interrogated by the police he believes he hears the person's heart beating louder and louder under the floorboards and that the police must hear it as well. This consumes him until he admits his deed and succumbs to the penalties. Obviously it was his guilt creating the sound of the dead man's heart. His own internal guilt and shame manifesting itself in what seemed like a circumstance he had no control over. How many times have we had a "Tell Tale Heart" in our lives? The aching guilt over something we did that hindered our ability to be at peace. We've all had something like that in our lives at one point or another and we either kept it inside, or relieved ourselves of the burden by telling the truth. Well imagine this same exact thing inside you today but hidden by your subconscious mind under rationalizations and excuses. Whether you allow yourself to acknowledge it or not, it still has the same effect on your psyche. Mark Twain said "The worst loneliness is to not be comfortable with yourself."

So the solution is to begin lifting the layers of denial, stop blaming our past for our present, and begin to become a person who deserves the things we want in life. We do this by ridding ourselves of guilt and shame and avoiding it in the future by being honest. This is something you can't fake. Remember, "The Truth" is inside you and it knows all of your secrets and it will not be tricked. In order to improve your life you need to actually become a person who deserves that life. This can only be done by first seeking out "The Truth" about you. Who you really are based on your actions not your excuses and intentions. Becoming accountable for your own life by no longer blaming your parents or anyone else, and changing your behaviors by questioning your true motives in all circumstances. Sounds like a lot of arduous work doesn't it? It is in the beginning, but it becomes natural and comfortable and easier as you begin to experience the fruits of your labor. The fruits being increased peace, joy, and happiness. It may also sound complex and confusing. But I assure you it is simply a matter of applying logic and reason to circumstances in your life and thus revealing and accepting "The Truth" regardless of what you may lose or not get. The tough part is that it almost can never be done on your own. It requires a trusted mentor and/or a wise and empathetic psychologist to question your answers and guide you through the layers of self-deception. I heard someone say "I cannot fix this brain with this brain". And of course, it requires you to have the willingness to accept truths you discover about yourself that you find distasteful so that you can change them.

No one is too far gone or exempt from making this change. From the violent, drug dealing, abusive pimp, to the employee stealing office supplies from work. Sometimes extreme circumstances and trauma the mind has experienced cause it to retreat too deeply from reality. It simply cannot or will not accept "The Truth" because the pain is too great, but it is never impossible and no one is out of reach.

Now that we better understand how and why we deceive ourselves and others, we can ask ourselves these questions; "How willing am I to apply logic and reason to my current belief system? Am I willing to see more clearly "The Truth" through my layers of self-deception in an effort to achieve true peace?" This can be a terrifying prospect, especially when the belief systems are tied to such deep feelings as religion, politics, family history and our perception of ourselves and the destiny of our souls. This leads us to the next chapter regarding acceptance.

Chapter Four
Acceptance

"I have not failed. I've just found 10,000 ways that won't work."
-Thomas Edison

Imagine a man who wants to fly like a bird so much so that every day he goes into his back yard and flaps his arms until he is exhausted. Defeated, he retreats into his house each night only to repeat the fruitless endeavor the next day over and over. Some might be impressed with his perseverance and yet others would label him insane. In any case, he renders himself frustrated, defeated and unfulfilled every day. And since the structure of our life is built with the bricks of today, that becomes who he is. Until the day he accepts his limitations, takes hang gliding lessons and learns he can soar with the birds aided by this peripheral.

This silly example shows us that acceptance does not equal defeat, but simply that we must find another means by which to accomplish our goals. Without acceptance we continue to repeat fruitless behavior and sentence ourselves to that limitation for as long as we refuse to acknowledge it. The man could have accepted his limitation and retreated into his house and wallowed in defeat and self-pity. Instead he accepted his limitation which freed his mind to seek and find a solution. This example shows us that acceptance alone is not always the answer but just the beginning. We can accept "The Truth" in a circumstance, but then what are we going to do about it? The responsibility this question evokes is exactly why we have such difficulty accepting something. The question "what are we going to do about it?" lurks in the darkness behind the door of denial and so we often choose to simply not open the door.

Acceptance is one of those concepts in life that is relatively easy to intellectualize, but is often so deep and profound beneath the surface that we struggle to really "get it" and apply it in our lives. You don't think so? Try this on for size; acceptance is _the_ key to happiness. That's right, it's that simple. People's suffering is inversely proportional to their ability to accept "The Truth". Everything you have read in this book so far has lead up to that simple point. But simple does not mean easy. Remember that door of denial is terrifying because the monster of responsibility lurks behind it. If I accept this circumstance for what it truly is then I am forced to take difficult action to resolve it and thus might lose something I have or not get something I want. Yes I know, there it is again, but as I said, it always boils down to that fear. It is often much easier and gives us short term comfort to deny the truth of a circumstance instead of accepting it for what it is and taking the difficult steps to correct it. For this means navigating through the short term discomfort in pursuit of the greater long term peace that is the gift of "The Truth". Often the denial is so deep that we require the help of a professional or a trusted mentor to lift the layers of fear and denial so we can even begin to consciously see it.

Acceptance can be misinterpreted and misapplied in your life if you allow yourself to use it as an excuse. If you say something like "I have to accept that my circumstances are what they are and just endure it" you are relieving yourself of the responsibility of making difficult changes in your life. I accepted that I was powerless over alcohol as a result of the chemical reaction it has in my body long before I was ready do something about it. Mainly because the short term discomfort seemed insurmountable to me and I couldn't imagine my life without it. It was easier to accept defeat and wallow in it than to actually do something about it.

Another example of one of the things we have to accept is other people. We can move a mountain with a teaspoon if we set our mind to it, but we will never be able to change other people unless they want to change. You may have a toxic person in your life, anyone from an annoying co-worker to one or both of your parents. You may tell yourself you simply have to accept them and endure the abuse and the effect it has on you. This is only partially true. You do have to accept someone for who they really are, but the responsibility falls upon you as to what you will do about it. If this toxic person refuses reasonable requests to stop their negative treatment, you almost always have the ability to limit or remove their access to you. You certainly cannot change them, but you can change how you allow them to affect you or if they even have the opportunity to affect you. If it is a parent or sibling you may be thinking "I can't remove them from my life." Yes, you can. If they are having such negative effects on your peace, you do have that option. The question is: are you willing to be true to yourself and take that difficult step with all its ramifications? In most cases they will try to draw you into their negativity for a while. But if you stand your ground eventually they will be forced to respect the new boundary you have defined and they may even start treating you better.

People throwing guilt, anger and negativity require someone to catch it. It's like a person alone in a field throwing a ball to no one, walking over, picking it up and throwing it to no one again. If you stop catching the guilt, anger and negativity they will eventually get bored of you. They will find someone else to catch it for them, but not before trying everything in their power to get you back in the game. Negative people want to draw you into their negativity. I know this because I used to be one and I loved the company when I could draw someone into my dark world. There's a saying I read on the wall a long time ago when I was in the military that stuck with me all these years; "never wrestle with a pig, you both get dirty and the pig likes it". It seems harsh to refer to negative people as pigs, but it is as true as true can be. If you repeatedly engage in conversation with a person who is angry, negative, demeaning, and argumentative, they draw you into their mud pile, you get frustrated and angry and they love it. When I was living in denial and blaming the world for my problems I was of course frustrated and angry. So I found likeminded people to sit in my mud pile with me and together we would pass judgment on all those dumb people walking around with those stupid smiles on their faces. Only when I began to accept the world as it truly was and myself as I truly was, and begin to take responsibility for myself and start to make difficult changes, was I able to slowly climb out of the mud pile. The people in the mud pile don't want you to leave them behind though, and they try everything to hold onto you and pull you back in. So you have to be determined to get out of it. And I'm here to tell you that I work hard and stay diligent to avoid ever going back in.

We may have to accept people for who they are, but we can decide what to do about it, even if it means a big change in our lives. Sometimes it is very painful to leave someone you love behind sitting in their mud pile begging you to come back in with them. When we do decide to stop lying to ourselves and accept "The Truth" we try to help others do the same, but ultimately we have to be true to ourselves first. We must put our own oxygen mask on first before we can help our fellow passengers.

Some situations just simply cannot be changed or avoided and we must find a way to accept them as well. I believe that depression (aka the mud pile) is rooted in our refusal to accept a situation as it truly is. We can literally drive ourselves into mental illness with frustration by expecting someone or something to change when they or it cannot be changed, something unchangeable such as the past for instance.

We only have one direction available to us in this world, and that is forward. We simply do not have the ability to go back in time and change something that has already happened. We all know this to be true on a conscious level and that it is a fact of our existence. But how many of us relive a moment in the past over and over in our heads trying to somehow change it when it can never be changed? We simply refuse to accept that it cannot be changed and drive ourselves mad with regret living it over and over. The ability to accept the past, correct the result of the circumstance if possible and move forward free of its hold on us is a beautiful ability we have at our disposal. And we always have that at our disposal. So why is it so difficult? The answer is our built in judge, jury, and executioner wants to punish us for our real or perceived guilt and will not let us off the hook so easy. So the process is; we accept that something happened and that we can't change it, we admit it and atone for our part in it as best we can, and then we forgive ourselves and try not to do it again. That is the recipe for peace.

I knew a man a long time ago who seemed to be at peace and willing to help others and living a good life. Then I found out that he had passed out at the wheel of a car while drunk and rear ended another car with a family in it killing the mother and child. He shared with me the journey of horrible shame and guilt and attempted suicides, to a place of peace and acceptance. This was a difficult journey for him, he didn't let himself off the hook and as a result he suffered immensely. Not as much as the survivors of that family, but he did suffer. How can a person find a way back from that level of guilt and despair? He told me it was a long and painful road to acceptance. He finally accepted the reality that he could never go back and change what happened and that he could only go forward and spend his life being of service to others and helping them avoid his mistakes. And that's exactly what he did. It sounds so simple doesn't it? Just accept the past, forgive yourself and move on. It isn't that easy though is it?

Sometimes there is a circumstance that we have no control over and no part of which we can change or avoid. But even in that situation there is still something we can change; we can change our perception of it. Life is a game of perception and point of view. You can expose a hundred people to the exact same circumstance and you will get a hundred different reactions to it. Negative people will see it as negative, positive people will see it as positive, etc. I was watching a documentary on life inside a maximum security prison and a prisoner was asked what the key to survival was inside a place like that. His response was something to the effect of; the ones who can accept their circumstance, cut ties with the outside world, and adapt to the life on the inside are the ones who make it. It's the ones who can't let go of the outside world and accept life as it is on the inside that go crazy or kill themselves. That perspective is as true on the outside of prison as it is on the inside, just in a much less restrictive environment. It is those that can accept the hand they've been dealt in life, whether it is fair or not, and then choose to use the assets they have and create opportunities to improve it who are the happy ones.

I knew a woman with schizophrenia who suffered horribly for many years. She told me how she refused to accept the diagnosis, the stigma and the dependence upon drugs and as a result let it systematically destroy her life. She described her journey to acceptance as being hard fought and nearly a lost battle, but that she did ultimately get there and begin to work with a doctor to find a solution. After a difficult trial and error process they found a drug that worked for her and she has blossomed and lives a truly happy and peaceful life. She finally accepted her lot in life, fair or not, and only then could she work to find a solution and peace.

I have also watched many people with incredible advantages in life fixate on something that they refused to accept and end up destroying their lives, some ending in suicide. Their refusal to accept their situation and thereby continuing a cycle of self-punishing and self-destructive behavior commonly ended in their demise. More often than not their answer when questioned was "it's just not fair". Fair or not, it is "The Truth" and the sooner you accept it the sooner you can let go of it and move on. Life isn't always fair, and I'm thankful for that. For if life was truly fair, I would have been dead in my twenties.

Sometimes we can destroy our own lives to spite someone else. When said aloud that sounds completely insane and it is. It is insane behavior to attempt to punish someone else by destroying your own happiness and peace wouldn't you agree? Then why do you hold on to resentments? Holding on to resentment is exactly the same insane behavior I just described. It's like taking poison in hopes the other person will die. If someone has wronged you, either real or perceived, and you are holding inside you anger and resentment toward them, who do you think you are punishing? This person has wronged you, they took your lunch money in first grade, or they killed your family driving drunk. Every time you think of them your stomach twists into a knot and you feel the venom inside you. Do you think this hurts them? Of course your conscious mind knows it doesn't, so why do we do it anyway? Our ego won't let us forgive because we feel that if we forgive them they win. But what do they win? By you holding on to the anger and resentment they win a permanent place in your head and the ability to continue to victimize you over and over every day. By forgiving them you expel them from your head and free yourself of their grasp, whether they want to have that power over you or not. When we look closely at this truth, and if we can accept it as "The Truth", we can simply decide to change our perspective and as a result find peace. Nothing outside of our brain changes and yet look at the profound change we can effect on ourselves with a simple change in point of view. Once again, this is a simple concept, but not at all easy.

Occasionally we see a family member of a victim of a horrible crime saying they forgive the person who perpetrated the horrible act. I used to think they were weak little sheep letting the wolves of the world just victimize them. I would say to myself "I'm no sheep, I'd hunt that bastard down and kill him slowly if he did that to someone I loved, that'll teach him." But now I see the courage, strength and unbelievable emotional and spiritual development it takes to offer forgiveness instead. How empowering it is for that person to not allow the horrible act to take the love and peace from their heart, and thus not allow them to be victimized twice with one crime. The ability to pause and apply logic, reason, and acceptance to a situation, and not allow unreasonable emotions to control us gives us incredible power and control over our own destiny. It is not weakness, it is exactly the opposite.

Make no mistake here; if someone kicked my door in and threatened my family I would fight with any means necessary, I am no one's doormat. My point is that once something has happened and we can no longer affect the outcome, we can choose anger and vengeance, or peace and love and clearly see who benefits from the choice we make. This may sound like some esoteric spiritual self-help practice, but it is simply the result of applying logic and reason to a situation, seeing "The Truth" in it, accepting it and acting accordingly. Someone can take your money, violate or destroy your body, but they can never take your peace unless you choose to hand it over to them.

This line of reasoning can be applied to the death penalty we still employ in some locations in the United States. Let's forget the practical fact that we can and have made mistakes in our judicial system and wrongly taken someone's life. Let's set aside the irrefutable fact that it is not a deterrent that has proven to lower capital crimes where it has been enforced. And finally let's disregard the fact that the appeals process and excess care it takes to maintain a death row inmate is more expensive than life imprisonment. The usual illogical and emotional response is "I don't care, they deserve to die for what they did." But if we can find the courage to lift the layers of emotion, self-deception and rationalization it is clearly no other motivation than vengeance. Vengeance which we think will give us satisfaction. But as we discussed in the previous paragraph, it only allows us to be victimized a second time by the perpetrator because we have darkened our own heart with hate.

Have you ever seen the family of the victim after the perpetrator has been put to death and noticed a restored peace and love in their hearts? You may see a hateful smile of retribution and vengeance satisfied, but you will not see true peace and love restored to their broken hearts. What you see is more pain and darkness perpetuated through a second violent act to answer the first one. I am not looking at this from some lofty spiritual perspective of forgiveness, just the logical practical "Truth" of it. Murder by any other name is still murder and hate begets hate and does not advance us toward peace as a civilization. If the death penalty were a real deterrent for violent crime and restored peace, joy, happiness and love into the hearts of the victims and their families, I would by all means say "kill em all." But it simply doesn't and we continue to do it as an illogical and emotional response to appease vengeance. When hate begets hate, hate wins. When hate begets love and forgiveness, hate loses.

The details aren't important from one case to another. And the severity of denial and acceptance varies and thus the depth of the destructive behavior varies, but the result is always the same. Those who are willing to see "The Truth" accept it and take responsibility for making the difficult changes it implies, are the ones who find the true peace that money, material assets, sexual conquests, revenge and power simply cannot provide.

I'm not suggesting we remove emotion from our life and act like robots, or like Mr. Spock on Star Trek. The illogical effect emotion has on us is what makes us all unique and beautiful and creative. But we can learn to see when it is causing self-destructive behaviors and build a balance of emotion and logic that works for us. Was it logical thinking or illogical thinking that made the Wright Brothers believe they could defy gravity and fly? I would say it was the illogical dream that it could happen that sparked the practical and logical process of achieving it.

In the following chapters we will look at how some commonly accepted illogical thinking effects our perception of some issues as a culture and a species. These topics are controversial and usually avoided because they touch people on such a deep and personal level. But we're going to dive in and pick the scabs and test our own belief systems under the scrutiny of logic and reason, and we may not like what we find. The following chapters are not for the faint of heart and if you continue reading you are about to find out how open minded you actually are.

Chapter Five
Family

"The last step in parental love involves the release of the beloved; the willing cutting of the cord that would otherwise keep the child in a state of emotional dependence."

-Lewis Mumford

The modern family dynamic is rapidly evolving, and as far as parenting goes, I don't believe there is such thing as a perfect way to do it. I also believe children are very resilient and can handle mistakes along the way, even big ones, and come out healthy and happy. But with that said, there is an epidemic in our Western civilization of grownup children in adult bodies as a result of either neglect or over protection. The result of both is just a different variation of the same outcome; grownups with childlike self-centeredness that retards emotional growth.

I am not going to speak on this topic from the perspective of how you the reader may want to raise your children, but more from the perspective of how our parents raised us and the evolution of the modern family dynamic. Considering the fact that I don't have children and my only credible point of view is that of an adult child who had to overcome poor parenting, I believe that is best. Besides, I can't imagine a parent listening to a single word about raising children from someone who doesn't have any.

In the 1970s and 1980s most households were two income situations for the first time in our history. Woman only joined the major workforce in great numbers after the feminist movement of the 1960s and the family dynamic changed almost immediately. I was a child of the 70s and 80s and almost every one of my friends and I came home to empty houses after school. We were essentially left to our own devices and our exhausted parents would come home late in the evening and wouldn't have a great deal of energy to deal with us properly. In a lot of cases there was love and all of the basic needs of life, but the ability for the parents to pay close attention to who their children were becoming was diminished. In many other cases there was outright abuse because it is much easier when you're tired to just hit a child than to take the time to reason with them. In any case and from whatever situation you came, our civilization has suffered and I will explain why I believe that is happening.

In the tribal communities of our past there was usually a clear and distinct progression for a child to take from infancy to adulthood, and it was understood and adhered to. An infant boy is nurtured by the mother and protected by her until he comes of age. At that point the men would begin to include him in their duties and he was shown what he was expected to be responsible for as he became an adult. He was shown that childish things were to be left behind. He would experience the painful but necessary lessons as he learned self-confidence as a result of trying and failing to keep up with the men until he slowly grew more capable. The days of being coddled by his mother were over, she knew it, the men knew it, and he would learn it quickly. The tribe expected him to become a responsible man and protect and provide for his family and the weaker members of the tribe. It didn't mean he could no longer have fun, just that his fun was no longer to be childish and self-serving.

A girl was raised by the women and taught what was expected of her as a young woman, and those roles were clearly defined. Her nurturing and emotional perspective was crucial to balancing the logical and fact based thinking of the men. The children would not have survived if not for the women. It was a perfect balance and absolutely required for our species to survive and develop.

As our civilized world progressed and industrialized, technology allowed us to be more comfortable and our lives became more complex. The defined roles of women and men became less clear as the requirements changed. That is completely normal and I expect us as a civilization to adapt as we progress. We certainly don't need to hold on to old rituals that are no longer relevant to our lifestyle. We should and will get to a point where the roles might be interchangeable and everyone will be comfortable with whatever choice a person makes for their own life. But for the last fifty years and for maybe the next fifty years we are in a confusing and uncomfortable transition period. Women are enjoying the freedom of personal choice, and they are paying the price for it as well. Heart attacks are dramatically up for women over the last fifty years. They are experiencing the pressure of making a living and competing in the workforce and raising children on their own in some cases. Men are benefitting from learning to express their softer side and getting in touch with their feelings and emotions, and they are paying the price for that as well. Their self-esteem can suffer as they learn to curb their aggression as society forces them to get along in a more emotional world.

I want to take this opportunity to remind you of the hard fought battle it was and is for women to take their place in our society. Women were treated as property for many generations being essentially held hostage and forced to accept a life they didn't want. Men covered them up and hid them away because they feared their own inability to control themselves and thus other men's ability to control themselves. They were blamed when men forced themselves on them and as a result of this torturous life some women would literally go insane. And what did men blame it on? They blamed it on their femininity of course. To solve the problem they would actually perform hysterectomies against the woman's will in an effort to calm them down thus the term "hysterical". It was common for men to beat women as if they were incorrigible children. It was legal for the men to beat their wives as long as the stick they beat them with was no larger in diameter than their own thumb, thus the term "rule of thumb". There is debate as to that being the origin of the term, but nonetheless English common law before the reign of Charles II permitted a man to give his wife "moderate correction." It was despicable, and is still happening in many parts of the world. In Africa and the Middle East women have their clitoris cut off to curb their sexual desires. They are forced to cover themselves so men won't be tempted by them and are subjected to many other atrocities.

I remind you of this because it is important to remember the hard fought battle women have had, and still have, to be respected, heard and understood. We are in the infancy of true equality, and this past experience is relative to our current dilemma of trying to overcome our instincts as we move forward in an attempt to better understand each other. We must remember where we came from in order to know where we're going.

We are adapting but we are still victims of our natural instincts. Necessary instincts that helped us get through the barbaric and brutal stage of our early development as a species. We are so quick to forget that men were supposed to be aggressive in a time when physical strength meant survival. Men had to make hard, cold, sometimes violent decisions based on logic and reason and not emotion. We forget that women were supposed to be nurturing and emotional and submit to the man's choices for the family. In the early stages of humanity there wasn't an atmosphere of comfort and safety to have family meetings and debate a course of action for the family. It's not easy for men or women to ignore those natural instincts and overcome them as we evolve. Men are intimidated by powerful women, or even a wife who makes more money than them. Women leaders in business and government feel the need to take on masculine traits in order to get men to respect them and follow their lead. Costa Rica President Laura Chinchilla, the country's first female leader, said in a Forbes interview that successful women face typecasting largely because society is still adjusting to women's recent decision-making power. Chinchilla believes the most pervasive stereotype is that women are "weak," a perception that may stem from women's greater desire to build a consensus. "We understand success not as the result of just one person but as the result of a team," she said. "[It's a] different way of dealing with power [that] is misunderstood as a kind of weakness."

Eventually each of us might become a perfect balance of emotion and logic, aggression and compassion and sex will no longer affect how we approach a situation, each of us having become the best of both. But until then, we struggle to deal with each other. Should a man open a door for woman? Fifty years ago there was no question about it, but you will receive mixed responses today. A woman might say thank you, or she might tell you she can open her own damn door and she doesn't need you. I'm not judging either response, just illustrating how we are all still a little confused about how to treat one another at the moment.

Is it any surprise at all that statistically the typical marriage has a 50/50 chance of success? In fact, how we define a successful marriage is even changing. Many people, men and women, will say if you stayed together 20 years and raised some healthy kids and then decided to go your separate ways that it was a successful marriage. According to 2010 Estimates from the Pew Research Center 52% of people under the age of 30 report having a step relative and 44% report having a step- or half-sibling, compared with 45% and 35%, respectively, of those age 30 to 49 which indicates we are still moving in the wrong direction. And these statistics don't paint the full picture because to date government reporting of population figures only indicate families in which the child resides. So if the child lives with a divorced, single parent and the other nonresident parent has remarried, the child is not included in the calculations as being a member of a stepfamily. Also, children who are 18 and older or no longer living at home are not included in these estimations.

Many children spend their time divided between their mother's and their father's house. They have to adapt to step parents and all the nuances of both environments from week to week. If you can tell me what a "normal" family is or what a clearly defined role for a woman and a man is in a relationship my hat is off to you. But the most negatively affected are the children, and then those children become parents and their children are negatively affected. Many single parents feel guilty about their failed relationship and that their child is part of a broken home, and in response they try to make up for it by over-coddling the child. According to Dr. Tim Elmore the founder and President of Growing Leaders, an organization dedicated to mentoring today's young people to become the leaders of tomorrow - "we let guilt get in the way of leading well." He goes on to say "Your child does not have to love you every minute. Your kids will get over the disappointment, but they won't get over the effects of being spoiled. So tell them "no" or "not now," and let them fight for what they really value and need." He also says "We rescue too quickly. Today's generation of young people has not developed some of the life skills kids did 30 years ago because adults swoop in and take care of problems for them. When we rescue too quickly and over-indulge our children with "assistance", we remove the need for them to navigate hardships and solve problems on their own."

The typical single mother is faced with a much larger challenge than she gets credit for. According to family therapist and male development specialist Michael Gurian in an article by Mikki Morrissette, "Males raised in homes of single mothers are definitely at more risk for social and personal problems than males raised in two-parent homes." According to Gurian, "A mom with a father involved in the boy's life typically does not have to do too much to extend out beyond who she already is. If she is alone in raising her son, however, then she has to hold onto her own identity as a woman and try to extend toward the masculine." This is an extremely difficult path to navigate for her, and sadly even when the best effort is put forth we can end up with men who are absent of an example of what a man is. And thus the cycle repeats. If you are a single mom and you think I'm wrong, ask yourself why it is such a challenge for you to find a decent man. As a man I can tell you there aren't many out there. Even the ones I start to think are men of honor and integrity ultimately show their true colors. I have a very difficult time finding a friend whom I consider a man of honor and integrity.

This information may seem off topic, but I am pointing out these statistics and realities of our current family dynamic to illustrate the source of the childish nature of many adults today. Our generation and the generation before us have missed out on many of the consistencies and guidance that a stable family provides. As a result we are quick to rationalize and excuse our childish and self-centered behaviors which make it difficult for us to understand and respect each other as we evolve.

Women have fought for equality and only earned the right to vote a generation or two ago, they have to work twice as hard for half the respect and they become resentful. They have to be tough and stand their ground which intimidates most men and thus relationships fail. Often there is infidelity as one or both are seeking validation from a stranger. Women have to play a duel role, going to work and being tough and dealing with the sexist stupidity and then coming home and being the sweet nurturing wife and mother. Men have the same challenge. They have to be sensitive to people's feelings and subdue the natural aggression and then be the strong protector who makes a woman feel safe whether she admits she needs that feeling from her man or not. Men, generally speaking, have lost the concept of honor and commitment and a sense of self. They are forced to navigate the fine line between being strong and decisive while allowing the woman to be strong and decisive without being intimidated and emasculated. It is a challenging dynamic for both. Women want to be strong and decisive and have an equal role in the decisions while simultaneously wanting their man to be "in charge" and not a wimp. What are either supposed to do? How are they supposed to feel in this confusing state of emotional transition? Each is acting differently on the outside than they feel on the inside, which as we discussed earlier creates fear and distance between people.

Even in the midst of this chaotic transition I remain optimistic. I am a humanist and I truly believe in us as a species. Most of the major changes we have experienced throughout history resulted in a dramatic swing of the pendulum to over-correct and then eventually it coming back to a more reasonable balance. I believe we who have been here over the last fifty to seventy years have simply been experiencing this pendulum swing, the redefining of the roles of men and women in modern civilization. Women feel they have to take on masculine traits in order to be respected and men feel they have to take on feminine traits in order to be sensitive and neither is true. I trust we will find a balance and women will be able to remain feminine while still being respected and a man can be masculine and strong without being controlling and intimidating. Even though I am hopeful for our future, yet again I digress and need to get back to the topic at hand.

The immediate result of the disintegration of the old family structure and the redefining of the new one is that children are not growing up. They are growing older, just not growing up, and by "they" I mean "we". Yes you and me. I am not speaking from some pedestal of judgment. I am speaking from the experience of having suffered a life as a child in an adult body and the painful process of hitting bottom and having to start over again. That is not an easy feat, to realize that all of your problems are rooted in a childlike self-centeredness and that you will have to learn to grow up in an adult body. You may be thinking "OK, I have a few things I want to work out, but I certainly don't need to grow up." Maybe so, but let's take a look.

There are two very distinct situations in which someone can grow up in most Western civilized countries; suburban middle or upper middle class and poverty. The very wealthy are a small demographic and have their own set of problems that I will not get into here. The Suburban middleclass child has a very comfortable life by the standards of our predecessors. Meaning they don't have to hunt for food on a daily basis and they don't have to worry about a sabre tooth tiger coming into their open cave while they sleep etc. This safety isn't always guaranteed; we are still a very violent species and home invasions and abductions happen at an alarming rate, but generally speaking, we have a relative feeling of comfort and security.

There are many children who are raised in this situation with a healthy self-image and a healthy balance of security and self-reliance and are properly weaned from their parents and go on to live a rewarding life. These people are sadly in the minority. Usually the child is raised in a busy and chaotic environment and are handed food, video games, money and anything else just to keep them busy so the parents or parent can get through the day. They begin to develop a sense of entitlement, a belief that the world owes them something because they have not had to work for anything. Every team in pee wee soccer gets the same trophy whether they win or lose because we don't want to hurt anyone's feelings or damage their self-esteem. This has the exact opposite effect and is the result of knee jerk responses absent of logic and common sense. Losing and seeing someone else win is what drives us to improve. Winning as a result of hard work and dedication to something is the reward. The child goes out into the real world and wonders why things aren't being handed to them simply because they showed up.

If you think I am exaggerating ask anyone in a middle management position if they don't spend an inordinate amount of time dealing with the childish interpersonal immaturity that should have been resolved in grammar school. Children are living in their parent's homes until their late 20's or even into their 30's and beyond, and the parents wonder how they became so overly dependent upon them. The parents were so busy they didn't have time to teach them the difficult lessons in life that create a sense of self confidence and humility. They didn't have the energy to deal with the pushback children give while learning to accept the difficult lessons. The children are just appeased for the sake of keeping the peace. Then parents will say "I don't know why they are acting like this, we gave them everything." Well, that is exactly why they are acting like this. Dr. Jeffrey Bernstein, Ph.D. in an article for Psychology Today said "Adult children who remain overly dependent on their parents often are allowed to get into this situation because their parents enable them. Perhaps this relationship dynamic stems from parents who want to be needed." So the child grows older and goes out into the world throwing tantrums when they don't get their way and complaining that life isn't fair. The result is a child inhabiting an adult body that was never properly weaned from their parents. I understand this is a dramatic over-simplification, but accepting variations in degrees, it is in my opinion a chronic and pervasive issue in modern civilization.

A child growing up in poverty on the other hand may actually benefit from the closeness of a loving and supportive family. They may learn that the love and support is the most important thing and not money and power. But in most cases they experience the effects of anger and resentment and are not shown love and support. Contrary to the suburban kids, they are not given anything in the home, and they learn they have to go out and fight for what they want and take it. They also don't learn to deal with emotions and the basic lessons in life. They don't feel the support of knowing they can find refuge in their home when the world gets difficult. They often find that comfort in gangs or maybe less sinister groups of likeminded kids. They also grow up thinking the world owes them something, but for a different reason and from a different perspective than the suburban kids. They on the other hand are weaned too quickly and have to find a way to take care of themselves without being properly prepared for the world. Again an oversimplified description, but I would argue that it is pretty accurate within ranges of degrees and variations.

In both cases we end up with children inhabiting adult bodies with false self-images and low self-esteem, because sociologically we have failed these kids. Why? Because we ourselves were failed by society, and when these two demographics bump into each other the clash can be devastating. One has a childish sense of false security and entitlement, the other a sense of resentment and anger that these people shouldn't have what they can't have, and boom, a powder keg of anger based in fear and lack of understanding.

Aside from the issues of these demographics interacting with each other, it creates major social instability within the demographics. Two children in adult bodies going through the motions of life they are told is expected of them. The path of school, work, relationship, marriage, kids is laid out for them. They are never taught to discover themselves and think for themselves. Slowly they create false images of themselves based on fear of being found out and not understanding why they can't relate to each other. They can't relate to each other because they don't know who they are themselves. They think they know what they're supposed to be and they pretend to be it. What you end up with is two fake personas trying to create a fake life that leaves them unfulfilled and resentful and afraid of each other. That is exactly at the core of the failed relationships; fear of each other resulting in a constant feeling of not getting what we want from the other person. Sadly what we usually want from the other person is for them to make us happy and fulfilled because we are sad and fearful. This is obviously a doomed endeavor, because no one else can make us happy or fulfilled. Two happy people meet and naturally improve each other's happiness. They support each other and nurture each other's happiness which is a fulfilling experience for both. But a happy person cannot make a sad and insecure person happy. As I described in previous chapters some of us are filled with fear and mistrust because we are insecure about ourselves. We don't want to be "found out" that the person we are trying to project to the world and to our partner isn't really who we are. But it terrifies us to reveal this self-discovery to our partners, our so called friends or anyone else because we will be labelled weak and a fraud.

I was given a very warped example of what a man is by my father, may he rest in peace. I learned by example that a man is someone who has many sexual conquests, expensive toys, intimidates people with his strength or wit and never lets anyone see weakness, or perceived weakness. Of course I followed this example, what choice did I have? But I found myself ultimately empty and unfulfilled. I was filled with guilt about how I treated people. I told my acquaintances about all of my sexual conquests to boost false pride and ego. I lifted weights and became strong and intimidated people because I felt small and afraid inside. I spent money beyond my means and told lies about what I had done and who I was. All to sustain the false image I was projecting to the world. I was hiding a scared and frightened little boy inside the big scary monster body I created just like the Wizard of Oz behind the curtain. Was this my father's and mother's fault? Of course it was, but whose fault is it that they were so damaged and unprepared for the world? Who cares? It doesn't matter because I finally accepted that I can't go back in time and change anything and it is self-destructive to hold resentments and blame. I am responsible to make the changes and take responsibility for myself and become an adult. I am responsible to stop the cycle of destruction from one generation to the next. The only difference is that I had missed the benefit of doing it as a child and would have to do it in an adult body.

This Freudian perspective that our woes originate from our parents, more specifically our mother, is just the beginning. Of course our problems originate from our parents or lack thereof, who could deny that? Positive traits are from our parents as well and that is just the nature of our development. So many of us are driven, well into adulthood, by a desire to prove something to our parents whatever it may be. Sometimes it's "I'll show you I can succeed even though you think I'm a loser", or "I want to succeed to finally win your approval and love." There are many variations and mixtures of this and some might say it is perfectly normal and acceptable. The problem is in defining what "succeed" means. Is money success? Is a long marriage with a family success and who's definition of success is it? How many of us reach a milestone of "success" and feel unfulfilled and disappointed because at that moment we ask ourselves why we even wanted it?

The worst manifestation of living your life based on your parents is the subconscious notion "I'll hurt myself to hurt you and pay you back." This is the most powerful because we are hurting ourselves and yet it is still driven by the parent's influence. Unable to directly hurt the parents the child does things to themselves simply because they know the parents will hate it. This can start them on a course of self-destructive behavior and ultimately a life lived that is not their own and they don't even realize it. Any life lived, good or bad, in an effort to prove something to our parents is not our own.

In all of these cases it is the result of a systematic failure of our society to properly support and then wean children from their parents.

Logic and Reason for the Rest of Us

In every case it is the parents fault and their parent's fault and so on and so on. I have seen many times a mom coddling a teenage son and treating him like he was a 10-year-old, mostly to serve her own needs as Dr. Bernstein suggested in the previous quote, and then in the same breath say that she can't stand these spineless men who don't stand up for themselves.

Yes it is the parents fault, and their parents fault and we could trace it back to our ancestors if we wanted to. But the moment you begin to "grow up" is the moment you stop excusing yourself by their fault. As I have said I was raised in an unhealthy household with alcohol abuse and violence and chaos. I subsequently self-destructed without proper guidance and closed many doors of opportunity in my life. I lived with that resentment for many years. I thought "I'm a smart guy, I was physically and mentally capable of just about anything if I had the right guidance. I could have been a surgeon or a pilot, and I ended up a high school dropout alcoholic because of them." That perspective allowed me as a child living in a man's body to rationalize and excuse my failures and behaviors until a single moment in time when I had an epiphany.

I was in a twelve step meeting and it was a general topic open discussion format. Someone started sharing about how their wife had cancer and they were forced to care for her day in and day out and that he was OK with that, but he never got to talk about how it affected him. Someone else shared about some very difficult burdens they were carrying and so I thought I would lighten my burden as well. I raised my hand and began to explain my woes due to an alcoholic mother, a father who was a drug addict and alcoholic and borderline agoraphobic, etc. and how these people affected me and what they had done to me. When I was done I felt better and I sat back to wait for the sympathy to come my way. I was 35 years old at that time still complaining about mommy and daddy. An old gentleman in the back raised his hand and said "isn't it funny how we can make other people's pain about us?" I thought, "yeah that's true, I hate when people do that." Then I realized he was talking about me and I was furious. My fists were clenched my face was red and boy was I going to give him a mouthful out in the parking lot. Then I started to see it. He was absolutely right. I made their pain all about me. My mother is an alcoholic, poor me, my father with his issues, poor me. And suddenly for the first time in my life my parents dropped from this pedestal I had put them on simply because they were my parents, and I saw them just as people with their own problems and issues. The childish sense of entitlement of what I thought they owed me fell away. I suddenly realized, like a giant key fitting into a lock and the tumblers all falling into place, that I had done that with every relationship in my life. I made everyone else's pain about me. It was at that exact moment in time that I cut the cord from my parents and what I thought they owed me. At that very moment sitting in a meeting I began to take responsibility for my own life. It was the beginning of my becoming a man. I had finally accepted that I was responsible for my own life and there were no more excuses. It greatly improved my relationship with my mother as well. I no longer judged her and expected anything from her, and I was able to see her with genuine empathy and compassion for the first time in my life. I saw her as just another person like anyone else in this world and she didn't owe me anything. It was the most freeing experience I ever had and I received it for a dollar donation in a basket from a former drunk. I have had many epiphanies, but that was a big one, and it all happened between my ears in a few seconds. Nothing but a simple shift in perspective and it changed my life.

Maybe your experience isn't that dramatic but if you are reading this book I would bet you have an unhealthy dependence upon your parents to some degree. You might be financially independent and not need anything from them, you may even help them financially. But if you get honest, how does that make you feel, and isn't that feeling still related to proving something to them?

This dependence can be the result of being over coddled and protected well beyond a healthy point. This serves the needs of the parent who wants to feel needed and not have to let go of "their baby". Usually an only child suffers from this excess of attention into adulthood, but it can be anyone. Sometimes the dependence is the result of neglect. The child spends their entire life trying to earn the approval and attention of the parent or trying to prove that they don't need it either consciously or subconsciously. If your parent managed to find the healthy balance between nurturing and ensuring independence, count your lucky stars because it is rare. There are varying degrees of these unhealthy dependencies, from the debilitating to the mildly frustrating. It is up to you to apply logic and reason to arrive at "The Truth" in your own circumstance and cut the cord.

If you are in your mid-twenties and beyond and find yourself still angry about what your parents did or didn't do for you or to you, this is unhealthy. It is very common so it may feel normal, but again that word normal is confused with common very often. Common does not mean healthy. If you find yourself repeatedly angered or frustrated by your parents because they do the same things they've been doing consistently your entire life, this is unhealthy. You expect them to change and believe that you have the right to demand they change because of what they owe you by nature of being your parents. You may have a great respect for your parent or parents and try very hard to live up to their standards. You may even seek their guidance throughout your life. This is absolutely healthy if they are not on a pedestal and you are living your own life with your own ambitions and simply asking for advice from a trusted advisor who happens to be your parent. Only you, by lifting layers of denial and finding the willingness to accept "The Truth" can determine if that is the case. Or if it is an unhealthy dependence and a grasp for approval that will never come.

We so often inherit negative mannerisms and idiosyncrasies of our parents and use them as an unhealthy source of bonding with them. Meaning we enjoy gambling with our dad, or drinking with our mom, or assassinating other people's character together. It can be any negative unhealthy behavior that we accept simply because we used it to bond with a parent. Or we find ourselves hating that thing about them, and don't realize that we are usually most passionate about someone's fault if it is a fault of our own. We hate most in other people what we hate most about ourselves. We can say "my mother makes everything about her" and refuse to see that it makes us so angry because subconsciously we hate that about ourselves.

No matter what your parental circumstance was and is the fact remains that you need to properly wean yourself from them if you want to take responsibility for your own life. Whether your experience was positive, negative, or even if you were abandoned and have only images of them positive or negative, this must be done. This means freeing yourself of any control they have over you, either materially or emotionally. This can be accomplished by applying logic and reason to the circumstance. They are just people like the billions of other people on the Earth, they are human, they are flawed, and they don't owe you anything. They influenced you and they sent you off in a certain direction, but as an adult it is up to you to become responsible and accountable for the rest of your life. You can follow in your parent's footsteps, positive or negative, or you can choose to go in the opposite direction as your parents, positive or negative. In either case you are still being influenced and controlled by them. It is a challenge to truly cut the cord, forgive them their mistakes, accept them as individuals and become your own person. That is an adult.

Chapter Six
God

"Men occasionally stumble over the truth, but most of them pick themselves up and hurry off as if nothing had happened."

-Winston Churchill

The word God in any language evokes many different and very deep connotations in every individual. Even if you are an atheist, it still evokes deeply felt passions and beliefs or non-beliefs. Everybody's experience with it and interpretation of it and how it affected their life instantly springs to mind when it is spoken. Our first exposure to the concept and how it was delivered to us, positively or negatively hits us like a kick in the stomach as soon as we hear the word. It touches us at our very core and we can easily become passionate and or defensive and even frustrated at other's passion and defensiveness, all with a single word. It affects us so deeply that most of us are very reluctant to even discuss the topic with people outside of our own belief system. Try that with any other word and see if it has the power that the word God does. Politics? Maybe, pretty close but not even in the same ball park. Death? Not really, except for the fact that it usually leads quickly back to the word God. Even I feel the need to capitalize the word as I am writing. Why is this word so powerful?

Let's apply logic and reason to it and see if we can navigate through the preconceptions of emotion to look at it objectively. I ask you to try while reading the next chapters to divorce yourself from your historic connection to the word God. I only use it for lack of a better term. In fact, in order that you can better remove these prejudiced conceptions of the word God I am going to use the term HP for Higher Power where needed so you can remain objective and I can better make my point.

I was raised an Italian Roman Catholic in New Jersey and also in a very emotionally and spiritually unhealthy environment. I was confused by what I was being taught in church and the hypocrisies of those teaching it to me. That, along with many other issues lit with the fuse of alcohol and drug use lead me in the direction to reject all of it. I was in so much emotional pain and turmoil and so confused by the world that created it for me that I couldn't believe there was any entity responsible for this chaos. I became an atheist and began to serve myself and vehemently rejected and scoffed at the thought of God. This perspective was ruled by emotion and anger and the childish self-centeredness of a frustrated teenager. Then I had an experience that I have only shared with a few people and it changed my perspective instantly. I'll share it publically in this book for the first time not to try and impress or convince anyone of anything, but simply because it is true and relevant to the topic. You can choose to take from it what works for you.

I was 17 years old and just got my driver's license and had just bought my mother's car. I now had the means to travel and explore and was always looking for a reason to go somewhere. An older brother of a friend, whom everyone knew had a very serious drug problem, asked me to drive him into New York City to pick up some pot. I didn't know this guy too well and I said I didn't have any money or much gas in my car. He told me as soon as we got the pot he would give me some and put gas in my car. So I agreed to the little road trip that would change my perception of the human condition forever. We drove into New York City and he directed me through many turns and circles. We went down this alley and that side street and so on to the point where I had no idea where I was and how to get out. I later learned we were in Spanish Harlem. He directed me to double park in a very scary neighborhood and that if he didn't come back in 10 minutes to just leave without him. Trying to be cool and pretend I wasn't scared I said "sure no problem, I'm cool." He got out of the car and ran into a dilapidated apartment building and I began to wait. I lit a cigarette and looked around and slowly began to realize my situation. I was a baby faced white kid in Spanish Harlem in a car I just bought from my mom with New Jersey license plates. In 1982 New York City I might as well have been a minnow in a shark tank. I looked across the street and saw some dangerous dudes eying me up in a park and I realized I had been sitting there for about 20 minutes. I was really getting scared and it suddenly dawned on me that I had no gas, the car was on dead E and I didn't know where I was or how to get out. Time was going by, 30 minutes, 50 minutes, an hour. The dangerous dudes in the park were circling and getting curious and I was in a panic. For the first time in my life I opened my heart in fear and in the truest form of hope I begged as an atheist "God if you are there please help me, please make him come back now." And then it got weird. At that moment everything went into slow motion. As soon as I had uttered the words he came running out of the apartment building. As he was trying to get in the car a guy came around the corner right in my view and stopped and was looking around at something. He was wearing a bright yellow T-shirt that said "smile God loves you" with the popular circle smiley face. Now keep in mind I was stone cold sober, but everything was going in slow motion like a movie at half speed. I felt something pass through my body that I had never felt before and have never felt since. What stunned me wasn't the circumstance or the possible coincidence that he came out right when I asked God for help. Or even the guy with the T-shirt stopping in my view at that exact moment in that strange location. What really got my attention was the feeling of a presence passing through my body that was pure love and pure peace and so powerful and beautiful and alive that I am welling up with tears just writing this. Time had stopped and I was smiling, dumbfounded, floating in the warmth of something beyond my comprehension. And then it passed out of me. I felt the weight of my body again and the harshness of this three dimensional world take hold. Slowly time sped up to normal and he was in the car yelling "GO GO GO, DRIVE". I snapped out of it, put the car in drive and floored it just as some thugs came running out of the building. As it turned out, the deal had gone bad and they wanted to kill him. As promised he put gas in my car, he gave me some pot and I never saw him again because he ended up dying of AIDS. But he will forever be a part of that moment for me. I tried for many weeks to rationalize it and convince myself it was just a weird feeling and didn't happen, but I couldn't do it. And from that moment on I knew there was a Higher Power (HP) in this universe. A loving and beautiful HP and most importantly that I wasn't alone, ever.

Even after this experience which made me an instant believer, I still didn't have faith. There is a big difference between believing in something and having faith in it. It took many years of anguish and turmoil and emotional pain before I could break through the "self" and begin to have faith in this HP that had touched me. But that is a different story for a different chapter. Even though I still had no faith, the undeniable belief in a creator made me put aside my stubborn emotions that were blocking the simple "Truth" that was evidenced by everything around me. When I lifted the veil of anger and prejudice I started to look at the world and began to see that all logic and reason defied the possibility that this is all an accident. That from nothing a sudden bang happened and all these particles came into existence and slowly formed these rocks we call planets. And that gravity magically occurred and created this protective bubble around this planet which created the environment for an ecosystem to take place where living things like amoebas took form and things turned into plants. And these plants just happen to take carbon dioxide from the air and produce oxygen. Then the temperature balances out because of a perfect orbit around an amazing source of light and heat caused by the nuclear fusion of hydrogen into helium by creating so much heat and pressure that the two hydrogen atoms pop together and become helium generating billions of tiny explosions that become the source of the light and heat at a perfect distance away. All of these things working together happen to allow the surface of this planet to warm and cool as it orbits this incredible source of light and heat so that the warming and cooling creates weather patterns that create a sustainable source of moisture. And then on top of all these accidents, suddenly from the goo arises an intelligent self-aware creature that can magically adapt to this environment as the environment changes. And that this creature is made up of atoms that are put together in way that it takes oxygen from the perfect air into these amazing balloons called lungs that transmit the oxygen through the body in this magical liquid called blood. And how about the coincidence that it even needs and can use the oxygen created by the plants? Could I disregard the accident that an unimaginable organ developed called the brain that can think and reason and learn and become aware of itself? That it can send electrical impulses through an incredibly complex circuit of things called nerves which stimulate these fibrous miracles called muscles to move in an exact and controlled manner so as to allow for mobility wherever this brain wants it to go? Forget about the likelihood that just accidentally this creature has these little orbs that can move around and take in light from that amazing source in the sky that just happens to reflect off of objects into these orbs and then is transmitted down these wirings called optical nerves and translated into a three dimensional picture of the world around it. All the while these orbs adjusting so the perfect amount of light enters in to compensate for an ever changing environment. All of which is wrapped in a water tight self-healing skin that can adjust its pigment and cool itself to adapt to various conditions on the planet. Well I could go on and on about hearing, the sense of touch and smell and don't even get me started on the coincidence that two of these creatures can come together and create another one which is a perfect hybrid of the two. And that the newly formed one takes on characteristics that help it improve its adaptability to the environment that just happens to have happened by accident, and that there even exists an instinct to compel them to come together to make a third. Ask me to apply logic and reason to all of this and arrive at the conclusion that it all happened by accident for no reason at all? That we just exist for a short time and disappear into nonexistence with absolutely no rhyme or reason? Sorry, I can't do it. Not because I need some false hope or incentive to carry on, but simply because it makes absolutely no sense. Imagine you are walking along the surface of a different planet. You come across a vehicle that was obviously perfectly designed to move around on this planet you are exploring and is obviously well thought out and extremely complex. Would you pass it by as just an accident that manifested itself by coincidence of the environment? Of course not, then why are some of us so quick to dismiss the well thought out and complex vehicle they inhabit as an accidental coincidence of our environment? It's illogical.

This mixture of experience and open minded observation is how I arrived at the conclusion that there is a HP of this universe. Not because I need to, but simply because it makes logical sense based on all the evidence around me. When I apply logic and reason to the circumstance of my environment that I am presented with, and I do my best to see "The Truth" by removing emotional preconceptions, I can't help but see anything but a perfectly planned out environment for these three dimensional vehicles we inhabit to move and exist in order to accomplish something.

There are many extreme points of view on this topic and it is my belief that "The Truth" lies dead smack in the middle of two extreme points of view no matter what the topic. Very rarely is any extreme point of view entirely wrong or entirely right. For instance there are the Darwinists that believe we are not the work of a HP or creator, just the simple biological effect of evolution. Then you have the

Logic and Reason for the Rest of Us

Creationists that believe it is not evolution, but simply the mighty work of HP. But why are we so quick to rule out a hybrid of those viewpoints? Couldn't it be possible that a wise and advanced being decided to put us somewhere in order that we may accomplish something, and thereby created this environment? And that it realized the vehicles we would inhabit would have to be able to adapt and change as there would be no way to anticipate how the environment would change after it was created? Is a giraffe's neck long because HP knew they would need to eat the leaves off of tall trees? Or did longer necked giraffes survive because they could reach the leaves and thereby mated with each other to genetically breed longer necked giraffes? The answer to both is yes. Maybe HP established the ability of creatures in this environment to evolve as required because it was a logical solution to an ever changing environment.

Imagine you go out to your garden and till the soil and prepare it just the way you know will be optimal for growing things. Then you take your tomato seeds and plant them fully expecting them to turn into tomatoes. You control the environment as best you can by shading it and watering it when needed and presto, the seeds begin to grow. They emerge from the soil and begin to use the Sun and water and nutrients in the soil to eventually grow into vines with big beautiful red tomatoes. Now imagine two of those tomatoes talking (yes they can talk in this scenario) and they are contemplating their existence. One is a Creationist tomato and one is a Darwinist tomato. The Darwinist tomato believes they have evolved from seeds into these beautiful red fruits simply by nature of biological evolution. The Creationist believes that a superior creature, you in this case, is responsible for their ability to become what they are. The two tomatoes fight and war breaks out in your garden and sadly all of the tomatoes die in the ugly war of the fruits known throughout history as The Ketchup Wars. But sadly they were both right, weren't they?

I have listened to so many heated debates between so called intelligent people with extreme ideology on a certain topic, and I am saddened that they have a difficult time seeing that "The Truth" is a hybrid of their beliefs. We are beginning to see the early stages of an open minded mutually agreeable perspective between scientists and spiritual minded people. Why do these two things need to be mutually exclusive? Science is nothing more than the pursuit of the already existing "Truth" of HP. Science isn't changing "The Truth", its changing people's perception of it as it reveals new facts. It was not long ago in our evolutionary timeline that men of science were put to death for contradicting the preconceptions and interpretations of religion. Sir Isaac Newton was shunned and ridiculed for his rejection of religious dogma in pursuit of uniting knowledge and belief.

Eventually we will arrive at a unity between the logic and reason of science and the logic and reason of spiritual matters concerning HP and why we are here. I know this simply because they are one in the same. The two are real, unavoidable, and all evidence indicates that our increased understanding of them is leading them full steam toward each other. They will collide in a perfectly logical coexistent and codependent explanation like puzzle pieces fitting together. Why wouldn't HP put the world together in a logical and reasonable way? And why does our lack of understanding of it lead us into mystical, illogical and unreasonable explanations of it? We find it so difficult to simply accept that we don't understand the logic of it yet but that we probably will someday.

We need to be patient as we discover things that lead us closer to "The Truth" progressively minimizing our ignorance. But no, we as humans have to label and categorize things into unreasonable packages that our little minds can comprehend and explain, thereby leading us to quarrel over explanations that are based in little or no fact at all. Why do we need to categorize and label everything? Well, based on a study led by a neuroscience doctoral student at the

University of California, Berkeley, they were able to visualize how the human brain stores information. The researchers found that, for instance, the brain organizes the categories of "humans" and "animals" in a related manner, whereas "eyeball" and "car" are stored in completely different areas of the brain. Along with finding out how the brain organizes different categories of objects, the researchers also found out that different people's brains organize things in similar ways. This leads me to conclude that in order to get information into our brains we must label and categorize it. We have to encapsulate information into an understandable framework and catalog it or our perception of the world around us would be abstract. This chaos would be equivalent to insanity in most human brains. This is good, this quality fuels our desire to understand ourselves and our world and make sense of it, but it makes it very difficult for us to accept what we can't understand yet.

We are also very quick to separate science from nature because we see nature as separate from ourselves. Humans tend to observe "nature" from outside of it forgetting that they are part of it. You can never see something accurately when you are seeing it subjectively and convincing yourself you are seeing it objectively. How quickly would you categorize plastic or chemicals as unnatural? We, with our brains and our little opposing thumbs and fingers created plastic and chemicals. Therefore they are as natural as a dam made by a beaver that turns a stream into a pond. We and everything we have done to this planet are as natural as a spider eating a bug. We have the advantage of being self-aware though, and so we can see what we are doing and make corrections. But the actions, the corrections, and the results are all part of nature. Our science only reveals that to us more and more clearly.

So if we can accept that there is a logical and reasonable being, HP, which created this place and put us here simply by accepting the irrefutable evidence around us, what are we supposed to accomplish here then? What is the point to all of this? We will apply logic and reason to that question in another chapter, but first we will examine the phenomenon of religion.

Chapter Seven
Religion

"I do not feel obliged to believe that same God who endowed us with sense, reason, and intellect had intended for us to forgo their use."

-Galileo

From the beginning of man when we were all scattered about the planet, congregated in little groups and isolated on different continents, we all had one thing in common. We all felt the presence of something bigger than ourselves controlling things, and I don't mean a sabre tooth tiger. Virtually every single group of humans, completely disconnected from one another, had this exact same "feeling". They couldn't articulate it or comprehend it, but they all had it. We know this because of cave drawings and artifacts left behind. Throughout the world we find Paleolithic Cave Art and in many of these caves, such as the Gargas caves in France, there appears to be a religious influence behind the art. So what were these ancient humanoids doing? They were interpreting the feelings as best they could in their own image and to suit their own needs. What else could they do? They tried to make sense of it and so with limited objectivity began to form stories and explanations for what they were seeing and feeling around them. Our species, like any species, has natural leaders and natural followers and there is nothing wrong with either, it's just a logical instinctual requirement to organize. You can't have everyone thinking they're in charge any more than everyone standing around not knowing what to do. So leaders emerge and followers congregate the same as bees, ants and birds. The leaders naturally began to share their limited understanding and attempts to make sense of everything. The followers thinking the leaders are special and must know something they don't know believed them.

The leaders quickly gained confidence and realized they could scare and control the followers with these stories. Mainly because these things around them, the Stars, the Sun, lightning and rain, were so big and powerful and mystical and most importantly, open for interpretation. The leaders were able to convince the followers, and usually convince themselves that they were getting the message from the great HP and were the conduit to the followers. Remarkably this has not changed at all in many thousands of years, but I digress yet again.

This would all be a perfect situation in which everyone fell into their place and became comfortable with the commonly understood beliefs and interpretations of the omnipotent HP. Harmony and peace would be our destiny as a species. But someone invented a boat and then it got real interesting. They set out across the sea to discover more of this strange world they lived in. And of course they encountered another group of people who had done the same exact thing they had done. This group also felt a HP but interpreted it in their own image. The problem is that those two interpretations were different. Upon discovering this difference it only made sense that if one was right the other must be wrong. And yet a third group of people set out in their boat and encountered yet another group all with their own interpretations of the same energy coming from the same HP. But who would concede? Sadly, no one would concede and thus began the wars of religion. These beliefs and interpretations were deeply held and had already been passed down through generations at that point. They were not going to be dismissed simply because another group had mistakenly interpreted the HP. Each group was terrified for the salvation of their souls and that their HP would punish them with sickness or famine if they did not defend his name. The leaders had told them that they would be punished if they didn't obey the HP. Each group had different names and identities for HP, and they all believed their version needed to be defended lest some of their own people be tricked into this other false belief and their soul lead astray from salvation. So they fought and killed each other and died with glory defending their ignorant interpretations of the same HP.

Does that scenario sound silly to you? It does to me, but that is exactly what happened. It astounds me that even today the most educated of our species can't see the profound illogical and irrational concept that the correct understanding of HP is based solely on the geography of their ancestors. Geography upon this tiny little rock we inhabit hurling through oblivion amongst billions of other tiny little rocks.

Imagine insects crawling around on a rock in your back yard. Try to imagine them fighting and killing each other because the ones originating on the Southern side of the rock interpreted you, the observer, differently than the insects on the Northern side of the rock interpreted you. Would you laugh and think them silly little ignorant bugs as they destroyed themselves? Why are we different from them simply because our rock is bigger? Ask yourself how it is logically and reasonably possible that your ancestors were right and all of the other ones were wrong. That in their misguided futile attempts to understand the same universal energy they all sensed, yours got it right.

A great deal of the fear we have of HP and other's interpretations of HP is based on beliefs passed down for generations. Beliefs founded on very little evidence we ourselves have seen or experienced. So we perpetuate the beliefs of our well-meaning but ignorant predecessors who also thought the world was flat. How is it logical that we can disregard almost all of the teachings of our ancestors with an empathetic nostalgia of their ignorance compared to our contemporary insight, and yet continue to blindly follow their religions? The answer harkens back to my earlier example of learning that water itself doesn't conduct electricity and that maybe our mother didn't love us. One doesn't affect our self-image and one does.

It is my belief based on logic and reason that there is a Creator of this place we inhabit. And that there is no one alive that truly understands it and truly knows what it wants from us. HP has no grandchildren, we all have a direct relationship to HP of our own understanding, and logic and reason dictates that we must accept our limited comprehension of it. But we want to believe that the priest, the rabbi and the cleric knows something we don't because he is special. Why do we want to believe that? Because we know that we don't know anything. And we need to think that someone does because we can't accept "The Truth" that no one knows yet. Anyone who tells you they know for a fact what God is and what God wants is either a liar or insane. There, I said it. Why is it possible that someone else has this undeniable conduit to HP and you don't? What makes them more special than you? Nothing!

Religions are, by logical definition, mass insanity. If you don't think mass insanity on such a large scale is possible, consider this: How long did you believe that Santa Claus was flying around the world in a sled delivering toys to only the good boys and girls? Yes, our parents used our faith in Santa Claus to control us and scare us into behaving just like the religious leaders do. And it was a deep and closely held faith we had in him. But you're thinking that was just a fun hoax that is perpetrated upon the children and is harmless. Did it feel harmless when you found out Santa wasn't real? Was it terrifying to find out that the entire world was in on a mass conspiracy to trick you? If you think I'm being over-dramatic just watch the moment when a child is learning that truth and the effect it has on them. It's on the news, there are people dressing up like him, the toys magically appear under the tree in the morning, very convincing. Do you think "mass conspiracy" is too dramatic of a word? You tell me what it is then.

Logic and Reason for the Rest of Us

Think about what would happen if no one ever told you the truth and the mass conspiracy of Santa was continued into adulthood. It would become even more believable because everyone else you know would be falling for the same hoax. The legend of Santa Claus was based on a real person who did very selfless things and helped people. The stories were told of him and his good deeds and of course they were enhanced and exaggerated as they were passed down. Ultimately the legend spread and he became much larger than life. Sound familiar?

This is the point where religious people start to get defensive and feel sorry for me that I don't have "God" in my life. I politely remind them that I have a very powerful and close relationship with HP accepting my limited understanding of it. I just don't subscribe to ancient dogma that asks me to defy all of the logic, reason and common sense that HP instilled in me. What I find most interesting is the ability of some religious people to pass judgments on the other religions. The one that gets picked on the most is the church of Scientology followed by the Mormons because they are more recently originated. But there is absolutely no difference between them and the well-established ancient religions. If a modern person came down from a mountain and tried to convince a contemporary religious person that the very things they currently believe in their religious books were happening right now they would lock him up and try to cure him. They might even say "show us proof of your claims", and sadly that is what I'm saying to them now. Ancient books written and re-written by men who thought the Sun was being pulled across the sky by a fiery chariot are no proof at all?

I know letting go of these things you have been taught your entire life that you believe can affect the way you spend eternity can be a very frightening concept. But isn't it really brainwashing more than teaching? I know the term brainwashing sounds harsh and might give you the impression that I take issue with religion, that's because I do.

Religions are the source of more death and destruction than any other topic in human history, including the famous "Ketchup Wars" in your garden. Religious people usually reply that there is much good that is done in the name of religion as well. Yes, that is true, however I believe religion has created far more turmoil, hate, and destruction in the human experience than good. Without religion, human nature would still drive us to organize and help each other, it just wouldn't be in the form of a church, synagogue or mosque etc.

These beliefs touch us at our very core and the thought of abandoning them terrifies us that we might be wrong and will be sentenced to damnation for eternity. That's called brainwashing. But I can tell you it is an unbelievably liberating and freeing experience to break away and open your mind to logic and reason and find a more common sense understanding of HP. Not the one your grandparents learned from their grandparents who learned it from their grandparents, none of whom saw anything to corroborate any of it.

If you don't think you can be brainwashed by mass conformation consider this scenario; you wake up one morning and there are two Suns in the sky and you are amazed and shocked. You run around and grab people and say "Oh my God do you see that? There are two Suns in the sky, what happened?" And the people calmly look at you as if you're crazy and say "my friend there have always been two Suns in the sky. Are you OK?" You obviously think this guy is nuts so you find others and they all tell you the same thing until you start to question yourself just a little bit. Then you go open a history book and see they describe the presence of two Suns in our sky throughout history and now you are really scared. How long do you think you could hold out believing what you know to be true? How long until you start giving in and considering the possibility that you have had some sort of a breakdown and must be mistaken? Reality is much more fragile than you want to believe. You should be getting used to my silly extreme examples by now and so you can see the point I am making here. That mass conformation is a very powerful and convincing force against the individual's own trust in reality. If enough people say the same thing long enough, we will begin to question ourselves. What I am attempting to do here is to enlighten enough people into the world of logic and reason that our common voice might make people feel safer to depart from the mass insanity and trust themselves again.

Keep in mind that I am not trying to convince anyone that the spiritual feeling and presence of a HP they have in their heart isn't real. I just told you a personal experience that happened to me in New York City that atheists would think was insane. I know there is a presence with us here on Earth and I am more convinced of that fact than most. My issue is with the adherence to archaic interpretations of that feeling. Interpretations that ask you to defy all of the common sense you have been bestowed with by that very presence you feel.

If you were raised in one of the Christian denominations you will interpret that presence as Jesus. If you happen to be born in the Middle East you would most likely interpret that presence as Allah. If you were born in areas of Asia you might feel it as Buddha. If your body entered this world in India by luck of the draw then you would most likely be brainwashed into thinking the presence you feel is Vishnu, Shiva, Ganesha, Krishna, Rama, or Hanuman etc., and all of the accompanying dogma that goes with each. Does this make any sense to you? That you take a baby born anywhere and begin the brainwashing and inject and shape his beliefs until he believes whatever you believe, and that as a result his belief must be true and right? Of course we become convinced of it, look at the time and effort that was taken to convince us. It's terrifying.

Here is where the extreme thinking tendency of the human brain comes into play. We have a very difficult time separating HP from religion. I tell religious people that the only religion I subscribe to is "The Truth" and most instantly jump to the conclusion that I don't have a HP in my life. It's because the concept of God or HP is so intertwined with their interpretation of it that it seems impossible that one could exist without the other. The only difference between me and them is that I accept that I have no concept of what HP is and that we are not meant to have that concept in our present form on this Earth. Just simply that I know it exists and I trust my "Instinct of Truth" that is in me under all of my fears and denial telling me what is right and wrong. I don't need to understand the genesis of it or encapsulate it into a story that my little brain can digest. I simply accept the variables in the equation as currently unknown.

Religious people I have encountered tend to find comfort in the fact that they're not personally involved in any religious conflict in the world. They tend to separate themselves from the global phenomenon of religious conflict throughout human history. But you cannot create a make-believe bubble in which to exist and separate yourself from the destructive, exclusive nature of religion as a whole. The single-most destructive concept in the human experience is religion, and you are either a participant in it or you are not.

Any Jew will be quick to tell you of the persecution their people have endured, and it will be absolutely true. But ask yourself why? If you read The Hebrew Bible (a term used by biblical scholars to refer to the Tanakh, the canonical collection of Jewish texts, which is the common textual source of the several canonical editions of the Christian Old Testament), the stories read like an amazing comic book of fire and brimstone and superhero angels where the Israelites are "God's chosen people". This meant that Abraham was chosen to tell the world that there was only one God and he knew who it was and everyone else with their Pagan deities were doomed to hell. If you want to piss people off and get yourself persecuted, just tell them that story and see what happens. Of course they were persecuted, they scared the hell out of everyone and alienated themselves by believing they were "The Chosen Ones". The stories that depict this beginning of man and God enlightening Abraham is so illogical and irrational and in direct conflict with all of the laws of common sense and physics that I simply cannot believe it has taken hold in modern society. If you don't believe me read it and see if any of it would make sense if someone were to tell you these things happened today.

I certainly don't need to single out the Jews. The Christians came into being based entirely on the belief of an immaculate conception of a baby that inspired three wise men to travel across deserts guided by a star to find the baby. And then there is no record of this amazing baby's life until he is 30 years old? There were tales of miracles performed by him, but we forget that people believed in magic and miracles long before Jesus started preaching. There were people standing in the market squares performing so called miracles of magic every day. It was not uncommon to mystify the ignorant field workers with magic. What separated Jesus from the rest of the pack was that he said he was the Son of God. The truth is we don't even know if that was what he was actually saying because the first gospel wasn't written until 40 years after his death. Until then it was just word of mouth stories of events that were exaggerated and passed on until they became larger than life just like Santa Claus. Try to tell me verbatim exactly what a friend of an acquaintance of your cousin's said 40 years ago and see how accurate it is. Maybe if we apply logic and reason to the situation, accepting that there was no more likelihood of superhuman miracles taking place back then than there is today, that Jesus was just an amazingly insightful and spiritual man. And that maybe he was trying to tell everyone that we are all the Sons of God; that HP has no grandchildren and you should find your own direct relationship with HP. I certainly would be a hypocrite to think I know that as fact, I'm just suggesting an alternate possibility.

If you are holding onto the concept of Jesus rising from the dead, just read the story and think about this alternate possibility; The Romans were pretty open-minded at the time, you could do and say and believe anything you wanted as long as you accepted Caesar as a deity. Jesus' crime was denying that fact and saying that there was a real HP and he was his son, which, by the way, I agree with. There is only one God and we are all his sons and daughters. But I digress. Jesus was brought before Pontius Pilot who was basically the governor of this little area in the Roman Empire. All Pontius wanted was peace and quiet and this was stirring up a lot of discord in his province. They brought Jesus to him and Pontius asked him to just stop saying these things and be peaceful, but Jesus refused. Pontius really had no issue with him. He tried to tell the people he wasn't really a criminal and offered up another criminal to them in place of Jesus. The Jews refused the offer and demanded his death. With no other choice and with no personal vendetta he reluctantly ordered Jesus to be crucified and he was. Jesus' family came to Pontius after the crucifixion and requested that they take Jesus' body for burial. Pontius replied as if he were surprised Jesus had died so quickly, wink wink. Because crucifixion itself usually didn't kill you, they didn't pierce arteries where you would bleed to death or damage anything critical. You would last for many days and die of dehydration and shock. Nonetheless Pontius allowed the family to take the body which was very unusual practice at the time. They took him off the cross and buried him in a cave, not underground where there is no air. Then, miraculously when the cave was opened he was gone. I ask you, if you remove dogma and generations of brainwashing is it possible that Pontius just gave him a way out of the mess he got himself into? Is it possible that maybe his family treated his wounds and he recovered and then "appeared as if in the flesh" before his followers because he actually was in the flesh?

Logic and Reason for the Rest of Us

We can smile lovingly at our silly children preparing for Santa and in the same breath look someone in the eyes and in all seriousness talk with a straight face about God telling a man to build a boat and collect two of every species and somehow get them all on board and cohabitating on this boat. And the purpose of this was that God wanted to flood the entire surface of the Earth (which is physically impossible by the way) so that when the waters receded he could start humanity over again. How can you tell me that the people who wrote that story have credibility in any other part of their story? These biblical stories aren't a buffet from which you can choose what you like and discard the rest, the sources of these stories are either credible or they aren't.

Well, eventually the Christians were persecuted and killed just like the Jews. When you tell everyone you're right and they're wrong about the destiny of their eternal souls you will be persecuted I promise you. I might be persecuted for writing this book. But what's even more interesting is that when the Christians did become powerful in numbers and had made believers of Kings, they went out in the name of Jesus on crusades of murder, rape, pillaging and plundering for 200 years. They left city streets literally running with the blood of the non-believers all the while holding beautiful crosses of gold in honor of Jesus who spoke of peace. They called it a "Holy War" which can be loosely translated in Arabic as "Jihad". And ironically everyone will tell you their religion is a peaceful one.

Muslims are no different and also believe in angels and that among the angels was Gabriel, who brought down the Quran to Muhammad and that there were many prophets. It quotes "Muhammad is not the father of any one of your men, but he is the Messenger of God and the last of the prophets..." (Quran, 33:40) It goes on to say "Indeed, they have disbelieved who have said, "God is the Messiah (Jesus), son of Mary." The Messiah said, "Children of Israel, worship God, my Lord and your Lord. Whoever associates partners in worship with God, then God has forbidden Paradise for him, and his home is the Fire (Hell). For the wrongdoers, there will be no helpers." (Quran, 5:72)

There is a clear and direct dispute with the Christians who threaten their belief and it goes on to say they will be punished "Indeed, they disbelieve who say, 'God is the third of three (in a trinity)' when there is no god but one God. If they desist not from what they say, truly, a painful punishment will befall the disbelievers among them. Would they not rather repent to God and ask His forgiveness? For God is Oft-Forgiving, Most Merciful. The Messiah (Jesus), son of Mary, was no more than a messenger... (Quran, 5:73-75)

It is amazing that they all say the same thing; my interpretation of HP is right and yours is wrong. If you threaten my interpretation you will be damned to an eternal fire and I may be forced to kill you in his name. Absolutely no different from the imaginary North and South insects I described on the rock in your back yard. They all believe that their messenger, Abraham, Jesus or Muhammad had been given the correct understanding and messages from HP and the rest are wrong.

Now I ask you, no matter what religion you may follow, is it logical and reasonable that an omnipotent intelligent being who wanted the inhabitants of Earth to find peace and know that there is only him and no others, would think it made sense to tell only one of us and hope this "chosen one" could convince the rest without being fully aware of the chaos that would cause? What logical and reasonable purpose would it serve to tell only one of us? Does it make sense that this HP would observe us after doing this like a child pulling the wings off of a fly enjoying the struggle we endure trying to convince each other that our messenger was the one he spoke to? That concept is just cruel and illogical. Does it sound like that process best serves the benefit of the omnipotent intelligent creator of this world, or more likely that it serves the messenger's needs?

Logic and Reason for the Rest of Us

I know many devoutly religious people and they are some of the most funny, intelligent and friendly people I have met. But every time I am speaking with a devout religious person, I can't help but think that behind this friendly personality is the belief that they know the one true God, and that in my ignorance I will be exempt from their salvation. If that arrogance doesn't promote alienation and persecution what does? We have just been programmed to accept it and so we all walk around smiling at each other with condescension, knowing that this poor slob next door to us is dammed to hell.

I realize I have just alienated most the world who are Jews, Muslims and Christians, and I probably haven't made many fans of atheists either. But it is time we stop being afraid to look at these stories under the scrutiny of logic and reason. It's time to accept that just because these events happened thousands of years ago does not mean they were any more subject to magic and miracles than we are today. Why are we so afraid to tell religious people that their religion makes absolutely no sense? I am certainly not singling out the Christians, Muslims and the Jews, the same logic and reason can be applied to debunk the genesis of any of the major religions. Why? Because no one knows what HP is and how we got here and there was no more magic back then then there is today. Imagine the religion David Copperfield could have started if he lived back then.

If you are a person who has subscribed to one of these religions you might be feeling anger, or maybe just a little bit of fear that maybe this is making sense to you. Or you might be feeling empathy for the damnation of my blasphemous soul, in which case I thank you. But see if you can, even if only for the sake of confirming your beliefs, try to apply logic and reason to your belief system. Then see at what point it requires you to depart from that logic and reason to sustain itself. The trump card most religious people always pull out when they are forced to abandon logic and reason in their belief system is

"Faith". They say "that's why they call it faith." Well, how can I argue with that? I can understand this perspective from the uneducated and ignorant, and I say that with empathy not condescension. But when it is someone whose intelligence and reasonable mind I respect in every other aspect of their life, and they can somehow abandon all of it in this one area of their mind, I am confounded. I know it sounds terrible, but I have a difficult time completely respecting someone who has dedicated their life and faith to one of these illogical belief systems even if they have achieved incredible things in other aspects of their life. We are told we need to respect people's religious beliefs, but how can I when they defy all the laws of common sense and reason I have?

Imagine you are listening to a professor of quantum physics at a reputable university and everything he is saying is unimaginably profound and intriguing. And then he says he has a little green space alien in his briefcase that helps him figure it all out but he can't show him to you because he is invisible. He or she may be the nicest person in the world and an incredible physicist, but don't they lose just a little credibility with the last part? If and when this book is published I will certainly lose friends and acquaintances, but hey, that's the price of telling "The Truth" sometimes.

Chapter Eight
Faith

"Faith is believing in something when common sense tells you not to."

- From the movie, "Miracle On 34th Street"

Does the quote above sound silly to you or make perfect sense? You might want to actually pause for a moment and really consider that question, because it is much more profound and deep than it may seem at first glance. Is it really a requirement to abandon common sense in order to achieve real faith, and if so, why? I would argue that it's not even possible. There is no way a sane human brain can have complete faith, in the true sense of the word, in something that defies its own common sense. There will always be doubt in something that defies your common sense, because there should be.

I have faith that our planet will go around the Sun again tomorrow and that as a result when I step out of bed gravity will continue to hold me to the floor. I also have faith that a HP exists and created this world for a reason, sorry atheists. Both of those examples of faith are based on common sense, logic and reason. When you ask me to accept something that defies logic and reason, that isn't faith, it is emotion trying to rationalize a false reality in an attempt to appease an irrational fear. A fear based solely in lack of acceptance.

I know that sounds cold and harsh, but "The Truth" often is. Not because "The Truth" itself is cold and harsh, on the contrary it is beautiful and reassuring from my perspective. But more that "The Truth" conflicts with your truth and invalidates your false reality.

Let's look at the profound difference between belief and faith. I believed that HP existed from that moment in New York City when I was 17, but I didn't have faith in HP until many years later. How many people will quickly respond in the affirmative when asked if they believe in a HP and the promise of salvation, and how many of them live in varying degrees of fear and anxiety in their everyday lives? Fear brought on by the fruitless attempt to control things they can't control. Faith and fear are inversely proportional and they cannot occupy the same space at the same time. I am referring to the belief in a HP of your own understanding and the faith that it is in control of the big picture. If this is your belief and yet you find yourself with feelings of fear, anxiety and frustration trying to control the uncontrollable, than logic and reason suggests you have very little faith in that belief.

That little prayer called "The Serenity Prayer" is so simple and yet so profoundly captures the secret to peace on Earth. "God (HP), grant me the serenity to accept the things I cannot change, the courage to change the things I can, and the wisdom to know the difference." Acceptance, courage and wisdom, these are the tools of peace, joy and love. This little book is intended to help guide you toward the last part; "the wisdom to know the difference." We all know there are things we cannot change and things we can change. Accurately defining the line between them is the difference between fear, depression and anxiety and happiness, joy and freedom. Depression is living in the past, anxiety is living in the future, and peace is living in the present with acceptance. Because the present is the only place we can actually effect change.

Everything you have read so far is my attempt to assist you in the life-long endeavor of accurately drawing that line between what you can and cannot change. Layers of self-deception and denial hinder us from accepting something we can't change. And so we suffer needlessly at our own hand with the frustration of trying to change it. The same self-deception and denial tells us we are victims, not responsible for and therefore helpless to change things that we absolutely can change. Resulting once again in us needlessly suffering at our own hand because we believe we deserve it. Self-destructive choices based in fear of losing something we have or not getting something we want rather than choices based on "The Truth".

When we work hard to change the things we can change and to accept the things we can't, and we have done it with as much honesty based in logic and reason as we can, then we can find peace in letting go of the outcome. Knowing that it will be exactly as it should be even if it's not what we think it should be. When you can do that, you have begun to know faith. But it requires the self-honesty that I have been harping on throughout the book.

When I look back at all of the things I thought didn't go my way and which ultimately ended up being exactly what I needed in hindsight, I learned to have more faith in HP each time. That is a difficult thing to do in the heat of the moment when you are in fear of losing something you have or not getting something you want. Whenever I feel fear creeping in I immediately ask the question "where is my faith?" and peace is quickly restored. But that ability was a long time in the making and is based on experiences of past causes, effects and outcomes, not irrational dogma.

If you just met a stranger, would you trust them with your life and your belongings? Of course not, it would take time for him to earn that trust and your faith in him. It is the same way with HP. You may have believed in a HP for a long time. But maybe it's time to break away from the dogma and irrational illogical stories, accept the reality of the world around you and the evidence you have in front of you, and actually begin to find true faith based on logic and reason.

If you have grasped the difference between "The Truth" and your truth and the many deep rooted causes for them to be different, can learn to accept reality and that the past is in the past and stop blaming others, forgive yourself, fight through the fear of losing what you have or not getting what you want, let go of other's definitions of what a HP is, work to continually be on the lookout for self-deception blinding you from "The Truth", you can begin to make it your lifelong endeavor to draw the line more and more accurately with increased wisdom between what you can and cannot change. Then you can find peace in this life no matter what is going on around you.

Based on all of the logic and reason I have at my disposal, the previous paragraph is why I believe we are on this Earth. Imagine you are HP and you exist in a place that requires a certain level of wisdom and understanding to exist in. You want to bring new souls in but their ignorance based on lack of maturity would destroy the very place itself. Just like you would be reluctant to allow 100 toddlers to run rampant through your house, they must mature and learn boundaries before they can earn the right to enjoy the refuge you have created for yourself. HP needed a place to put us and the means to mature emotionally and spiritually, a spiritual kindergarten for lack of a better term. Which brings me back to an earlier point I made, that life on this Earth is nothing more than an opportunity to grow, and that all of the ups and downs and challenges and relationships are merely props to facilitate that growth. So many of us get distracted into making the props the purpose of life, but they are only meant to create the circumstances for us to grow. So seek out discomfort, seek out humility and anything that will help you grow, because I believe it is your only way out of here.

Obviously you can see the similarity of what I just described and the concept of Heaven, but Heaven, like God, is a word that evokes historical images and emotional baggage. So call it whatever you want, but this process is the only logical and reasonable purpose for our time here which is in my opinion very methodically planned out by a very intelligent HP. This also answers the question people ask when horrible things happen in life "how could God allow that to happen?" Logic and reason tells me that we are given free will so we can learn. If HP controlled the outcome of everything it would instantly invalidate the entire purpose of our being here. I'm sure HP is saddened and hurt when one of us uses that free will for horrible purposes, but it is part of the process. It is also a logical conclusion that the human condition on this Earth in our present form will never reach a state of perfect peace and utopia, because the moment it did would be the moment it no longer had a purpose.

When you have worked hard and minimized or eliminated the fear of being found out like the Wizard of Oz because you learned to be true to yourself and no longer have anything to hide, you will find peace and acceptance no matter what lesson of growth you are faced with on this Earth. Because the lessons it teaches you bring you closer to graduating. The fear of death will leave you because logic and reason tells you that death is alarmingly similar to birth and is simply the entrance and exit process from here. In both cases it is reported that we go through a frightening tunnel toward the light. My advice though, is not to trust anyone who tells you they know what's on the other side of the tunnel. They don't know any more than you or I do and they are only trying to manipulate you.

Most people are so afraid of their own mortality and they want to preserve their body as if it is part of them. The body is not you, it is simply a vehicle you inhabit to move around in this environment. When it breaks down and fails you will get out of it and continue on your journey as you would get out of a broken down car and start walking. I don't claim to know this as fact, it simply makes sense.

I suggest you stop avoiding the thought of your inevitable mortality and the illusion of time and embrace it. As the famous poet Jim Morrison once said "no one here gets out alive." That is "The Truth" whether you have accepted it as your truth or not. And you are not guaranteed another day or another hour. Ask yourself every day "if my body died today am I at peace? Do I love myself because I act as a person who deserves my love? Do the people I love know I love them? Have I atoned for my mistakes so I am free of guilt, shame and remorse? Am I free of self-destructive resentment and anger that can easily be eliminated with forgiveness?"

When you have worked to apply the practices I have described in this book and get to a place where you can answer these questions in the affirmative you will have arrived at peace through logic and reason. You will no longer fear "death" because you understand that we are simply passing through this place briefly. And obviously we can take nothing from it with us accept what we learned while we were here. Who knows what's next? Who cares? We can't avoid it anyway and that's "The Truth".

If you stepped out of your house and got hit by a bus and were lying on the ground taking your last breath would you want to have wasted your last day here angry, worried and frustrated over things you can't know or control? No matter if you are reading this on death row or if you are a teenager just beginning your life, it is never too early or too late to discover peace through logic and reason. Maybe now is the time to reconsider the idealistic proposal I suggested in the beginning of the book. Do you see now that if everyone practiced the philosophy of self-honesty I have described, there truly would be no reason for one person to be pointing a gun at another person.

Physicists just discovered what they believe to be the Higgs Boson which might prove the existence of the Higgs Field. The Higgs Field is at the center of what they call their standard model of our physical existence because it may explain how some things have mass when they shouldn't. This is amazing and is part of the excitement of being human and the desire to explore. Maybe they are getting close to the edge of our existence and another existence, or maybe a trap door will open that only reveals another thousand years of questions. Who knows? I certainly don't. I only suggest that you base your image of yourself and the world around you on "The Truth" and not the irrational explanations of others.

Writing this has been very cathartic for me and I hope some of you will benefit from my humble perspective. I trust I will see you all on the other side.

It's only logical.

Love, Greg.

Logic and Reason for the Rest of Us

www.ingramcontent.com/pod-product-compliance
Lightning Source LLC
LaVergne TN
LVHW051658080426
835511LV00017B/2629